Confessions of a CPA

Why what I was taught to be true has turned out not to be

Bryan S. Bloom, CPA

Copyright © 2011 by Bryan S. Bloom

ISBN 978-0-7414-7191-8 Paperback
ISBN 978-0-7414-7192-5 eBook

Printed in the United States of America

Published December 2012

∞

INFINITY PUBLISHING
1094 New DeHaven Street, Suite 100
West Conshohocken, PA 19428-2713
Toll-free (877) BUY BOOK
Local Phone (610) 941-9999
Fax (610) 941-9959
Info@buybooksontheweb.com
www.buybooksontheweb.com

Dedication

To my extraordinary wife, Pamela, from whom I receive love, support, and inspiration to pursue the really important things in life. And to my children, Callie and Corrie, who remind me daily of the value of making investments in the generations ahead.

Acknowledgments

There are so many people who have influenced my career and encouraged me to write this book, all of whom have made this book possible.

First and foremost, I am grateful to my Heavenly Father, the Yahweh of the Old Testament of the Bible who lets me call him "Abba Father," and his Son, Jesus Christ, who is my personal Lord and Savior.

I'd also like to thank my wife, Pam, and my children, Callie Sederquist and Corrie Musgrave, for their love and encouragement to write and create.

My extended family has been influential as well: my parents, John and Jackie Bloom, and Pam's parents, Harold and Annie Jean Ray. Thank you. My first clients were my brother Jeff and Pam's sister and brother-in-law, Angela and Byron Boyd. Thank you for letting me experiment on you.

None of this could have been possible without the support of my friends at Chesser Financial. To my fellow financial advisers, Jamie Chesser, John Butler, Jim Lilley, Terri Wetzel, Rich Bloom, Tim Noice, and Scott Olthoff, thank you for helping edit the content of this book and for your ideas of what to include. The support staff at Chesser Financial can often go unnoticed because they do their jobs so well, but not here! Thank you, Bette, Chrissy, Cassi, Eric, and Christy.

i

Many thanks go to two people at Chesser Financial that I never could have done without: Jason and Sarah Fagan. Jason, you served me so well as my personal assistant that you saw the potential of helping others financially and chose to become an adviser. I consider that a compliment. Thank you for picking up so many pieces that would have fallen through the cracks without your unselfish service. Sarah, thank you for all the little things you do, which add up to huge things when I don't get them done.

I would be remiss if I didn't mention my "study group." This group of individuals has helped me refine my thinking about what I was taught to be true. Each time I realized another fallacy of traditional financial thinking, these guys verified my thinking. Thanks to Rich Wesselt, Ian Meierdiercks, Phil Bodine, Phil Cavender, Jon Cunningham, David Anderson, Tom Love, John Cush, Jim Lilley, and Jamie Chesser.

Finally, I'd like to thank some of my friends and inspirers from within the financial services industry. When I first started my independent career, Roger Pryor provided significant encouragement for me to succeed in my career. Professionally, I owe a debt of gratitude to Larry Adams, Doc Huffman, and David O'Malley, who presented me with the Chairman's Navigator Award in 2010 in recognition of "the highest standard of professionalism, dedication, commitment and leadership." I received the award during the one-hundredth anniversary of the Ohio National Financial Services; presented for only the second time, it is given to an individual "who is of exceptional character and integrity." Thank you for your confidence in me by granting me this honor.

Foreword

The longer I am in the business world, the more questions I have regarding who has our best interests at heart. Many of the things I was taught about money have turned out to not be true.

When are you going to find out? I met Bryan Bloom while attending an insurance industry convention. As we spoke, I learned of his extensive background as a private-practice CPA for twenty-five years. We shared some concerns about the new learning curve he must have endured to become so successful in the insurance industry.

Since then we have met several times, and I think I am at least as excited about this book as he is.

Our industry needs to be taught some key truths about money. What better way to learn than from someone who has stood on both sides of the fence? We need to learn that some of the things we do on a daily basis should be analyzed a bit more.

Once those analyses have been done, we not only see how they affect us, but also, and much more importantly, we can learn how to manage them from that point forward to *our* advantage.

This book is a *must-read,* and I am very privileged to have had a very small part in encouraging Bryan to write this book.

It is time we learned the truth! No matter what your age and no matter what phase in life you are in, this book will help you sort through the untruths, misstatements, and simple *fog* around achieving financial success.

From all of us in the insurance industry, thank you, Bryan.

Thomas Love

Contents

Miracle of Compound Interest

Compound interest has been called the eighth wonder of the world. Whether you are looking at the seven wonders of the ancient world, the seven wonders of the natural world, or the seven wonders of the modern world, many would add the miracle of compound interest as the eighth wonder. It has risen to such heights because the exponential curve it creates rises to heights that command our attention. It doesn't matter whether you save a single sum or a series of amounts; when left alone to grow, it grows exponentially. Then, not only do your deposits earn interest, but their interest earns interest as well. The potential is unlimited.

It doesn't matter whether you are saving for a child's education, your retirement years, or even to leave a legacy from your physical lifetime; the miracle occurs. Let's consider the first two of these, since this is what I was taught to believe about how it would work.

Suppose you were to have a child today and wanted to begin his or her college savings fund immediately. In order to have a sufficient sum of money available to pay for four years of public university education eighteen years from now, you would need to begin saving $9,000 each year for eighteen years. If you did that, you would save $162,000 of your own money, but your account would grow to $265,000 if you were able to earn 5% on that money for each of the eighteen years. The extra $100,000 comes from not only your money earning interest, but also from your interest earning interest: enough to pay over $70,000 per year for four years of Junior's education. Yes, that is a lot, but it is merely today's cost of tuition for a public university, compounding at 2011 increases.

At the end of the four years of education, the university now has the $265,000, and you have zero. Not only does the university have the money, but it also has the ability to earn interest on the money, which was once your opportunity. We call that transferring the parent's miracle to the university's miracle!

If you wanted to accumulate the magic retirement amount of $1,000,000 between your college graduation and age sixty-five— a mere forty-three years—you'd need to save less per year than you need for Junior's education. In fact, at an earnings rate of the same 5%, you'd need to save $6,660 per year. Why less? Because the retirement miracle has forty-three years to run, not just eighteen.

Let's combine these two ideas in order to further understand this miracle. If the college funding of $9,000 were to run for eighteen years and then that value continued to be allowed to earn for another forty-seven years, instead of transferring the miracle to the university, Junior would have $2,633,512 to retire on. Let's take it one last step: what if Junior added his own $6,660 to Mom and Dad's college savings? He could retire on over $3.8 million! Now do you see why it is called a miracle?

Some financial advisers would lead you to believe that you can earn more than 5%; indeed you might, and if you do, the miracle gets even better. If you can add just 1% to this last example, at age sixty-five you would have almost $5.8 million. Many advisers still believe you can earn 8% in the market over the long run, which would yield a miraculous result of $13 million. And if you listen to a popular financial talk show host, he will tell you that you can earn 12%. If the miracle grew at the rate of 12%, which would be even more miraculous than compound interest, you would have $67 million!

If the miracle of compound interest is really true, why aren't we all rich by now? Even if you earned 8% on a $100-per-month savings plan over your working career, you would have $450,000 at age sixty-five. Are you on target? If what you were taught to be true turned out not to be, when would you want to know? Keep reading.

Look at the following graph. This is $9,000 per year being saved for eighteen years at 5%. Notice that the graph isn't exponential.

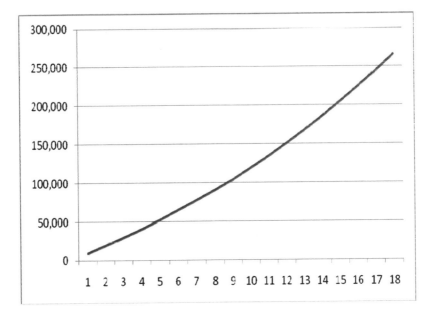

But look at the university's graph after the money is trans-ferred to it. Notice the linear nature of the first eighteen years, and the exponential growth after the money is in the hands of the university. I am assuming the same 5% rate of return.

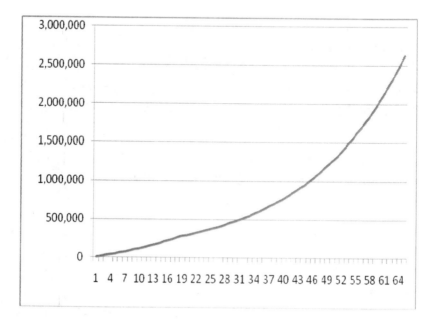

Lesson #1: What I was taught to be true about the miracle of compound interest has turned out not to be true, because there is no allowance for spending money during the compounding period. When we spend the miracle and transfer it to someone else, the compounding stops.

This lesson is compounded due to taxes. Even if we don't choose to spend the miracle, we may be *forced* to spend some of it to pay the taxes due on the annual growth of the account. If we don't pay it from the account, we have to compromise our lifestyle to pay the income taxes. Funds to pay income taxes due on the growth have to come from somewhere, either from the account itself or from our discretionary spending budget. If the money comes from the account, the miracle can't work, and if it comes from a compromised lifestyle, that doesn't sound like much fun.

Let's go back to the million-dollar retirement. Because Uncle Sam demands that you pay taxes on the interest and dividends you earn, as you earn them, the million dollars are stunted greatly. Paying a combined federal and state tax rate of 30% on the earnings, as earned, reduces your miracle to $667,000.

If you add up the tax on just the growth each year, the tax you pay is $163,000, *but* the miracle of compound interest is now working against you. Because the taxes due were extracted from the account, they were no longer in the account to earn the compounding interest. A dollar spent is no longer available to ever earn again; that is called *opportunity cost*. The opportunity cost of paying the taxes out of the account is another $170,000. Add the two together, and subtract the total from the original million you thought you'd have, and you end up with $667,000. Not exactly the million-dollar retirement you had in mind.

As fast as the exponential curve is increasing while interest is compounding, the taxes due and the lost opportunity from paying the tax are also increasing. The taxes due and the lost opportunity from paying the tax are eroding your compounding.

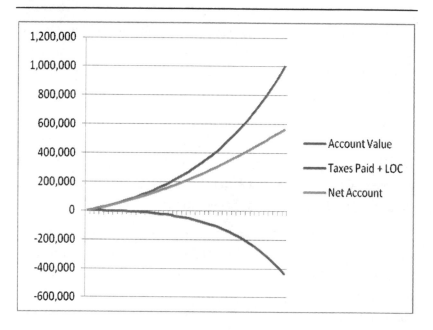

Look at the net account line; it is nearly linear again. The taxes stole your miracle.

Lesson #2: What I was taught to be true about compound interest has turned out not to be true, because the taxes due on the growth tarnish the miracle by reducing the amount of money that one would otherwise expect.

There is at least one more reason why what I was taught about compound interest hasn't turned out to be true. When we realize it doesn't work, we quit.

Let's use the example of someone who wants to invest $5,000 per year and actually experiences a 9% rate of return on his investments. Slowly, the account gains momentum, but by the time the exponential curve begins to take place in year eighteen, you realize the following:

Year	Annual deposit	Beginning of year	Annual "1099"	Annual tax due
1	5,000	5,000	450	-135
2	5,000	10,450	941	-282
3	5,000	16,391	1,475	-443
4	5,000	22,866	2,058	-617
5	5,000	29,924	2,693	-808
6	5,000	37,617	3,386	-1,016
7	5,000	46,002	4,140	-1,242
8	5,000	55,142	4,963	-1,489
9	5,000	65,105	5,859	-1,758
10	5,000	75,965	6,837	-2,051
11	5,000	87,801	7,902	-2,371
12	5,000	100,704	9,063	-2,719
13	5,000	114,767	10,329	-3,099
14	5,000	130,096	11,709	-3,513
15	5,000	146,805	13,212	-3,964
16	5,000	165,017	14,852	-4,455
17	5,000	184,869	16,638	-4,991
18	5,000	206,507	18,586	-5,576

You get to year eighteen, and you realize that you are paying more in taxes annually than you are saving annually. Why keep saving when all you're doing is creating a tax bill equal to the annual savings? It's a very good question, and you stop saving!

For those inclined to stop saving, the thinking goes like this. In the early years, it's not so bad. In year one, you are paying only an extra $135 in taxes. You hardly notice it, and perhaps it reduces your tax refund only at the end of the year. In year two,

7

the taxes are only $147 more than for year one, and again you don't notice. It is like the heat being turned up slowly; the cold water warms, it grows in temperature, eventually it gets hot, and before you know it, your goose is cooked, and what you are saving is being spent on taxes! As the chart shows, your account is worth over $200,000, but it is costing you more in taxes than what you are depositing each year.

Lesson #3: What I was taught to be true about compound interest has turned out not to be true, because when we realize the impact of having to pay taxes on the growth of our account, we may stop saving or investing.

Rate of Return

What is average? An average thing is something common or typical. When used to describe a rate of return, it is what can be expected to happen over and over again, resulting in a hypothetical projection. Expectations of the future are often based on what happened in the past, even though every investment projection you see states that "past performance is not a prediction of future performance." A common way of looking at averages is to calculate the mean of a series of numbers. The mean return over a number of years is the sum of the returns during those specific years, divided by the number of years you are looking at. This number is commonly referred to as the *average rate of return*. However you define "average," I've learned that what I've been taught about averages couldn't be farther from the actual truth.

Let's start with a fairly simple example. If you had $1,000 and averaged 20% return per year for two years, you would have $1,440 at the conclusion of two years.

An average rate of return is an easy and convenient way to project the future potential of a financial plan. Too bad it doesn't work. The main reason why average rates of return are a faulty way of looking at your finances is because averages are not actual rates of return, and the order in which actual returns occur can make a big difference.

Take, for example, the S&P 500 index for the period 1973 through 1997. During this twenty-five-year time period, the S&P suffered through some of its worst periods of time, including a single-day drop of over 22% in 1987, and one of its longest rallies during the 1990s. During this time period, the index had an average annual rate of return of 10.11%. Indeed, if you added up each individual annual return and divided by 25, you would arrive at the statistical average of 10.11%.
(*Source*: www.standardandpoors.com)

If you invested $100,000 in 1973 and actually earned 10.11% each year for twenty-five years, you would have the expectation that your nest egg would be $1,110,000. Unfortunately, you don't earn the same rate each year. So let's calculate what you would have actually had at the conclusion of those twenty-five years if you had invested $100,000 in 1973 and earned what the market actually earned year after year. If you had left it to grow and compound, you would have $821,000. This is a difference of $279,000 less than the average would have created!

Lesson #1: What I was taught to be true about rates of return turned out not to be true, because averages aren't what you actually get to spend and enjoy.

From what we learned in Chapter 1, what hasn't been accounted for yet? That's right—taxes. Average rates of return—in fact, actual returns as well—are never reduced for taxes when they are disclosed to you. Those typical mountain charts that you are provided every time you purchase a mutual fund assume you are paying the taxes on the growth of the fund from your lifestyle.

What if the taxes due were netted out of the account instead of out of your standard of living? Let's consider a hypothetical mutual fund with a seventy-six-year history. Without netting the taxes out of the fund balance, the marketing piece would show that $10,000 invested in the fund in 1934 would grow to almost $58.5 million if you reinvested the dividends paid by the fund. Rarely would the fund marketing material indicate that the taxes due each year on the growth of the fund were paid by the investor's "other" money to make the numbers and graph work. If you netted the taxes from the fund, assumed to be 30% of the fund's income return and 15% of its capital gain return, your $10,000 investment seventy-six years ago would be just shy of $8.9 million today. That is 84% less than what you are led to believe from the fund's growth chart.

Lesson #2: What I was taught to be true about rates of return has turned out not to be true, because taxes take a large portion of my expectations away.

Now that you have a good feel for why what we are taught about rates of return isn't necessarily true, let's finish with the fairly simple example we started with. By now, you are probably thinking that what seems to be simple may not be. Our example was that an investment of $1,000 that averages 20% over two years would yield $1,440. But might it also yield the following:

$1,280? It sure will. An extremely volatile market that earns 60% in the first year and then loses 20% the second year has an average rate of return of 20% and an account value of $1,280, not $1,440.

$800? Of course not. How can you average a positive rate of return and end up with less money? There once was a time, not too many years ago, that you could purchase an unbuilt home and sell it for twice what you paid for it before you moved in. That is a 100% return. Shortly thereafter, that same property fell 60% in value. Over the two-year period, the average rate of return was 20%, yet you have less money.

11

$0? Now you know this is a trick question, but again it is true. You can average 20% for two years and yet lose all of your money. Anyone who earns 140% and then loses it all—that is, 100%—ends up with $0, and yet averages 20%.

Lesson #3: What I was taught to be true about rates of return and has turned out not to be true is that how much money you end up with is more important than any rate of return. Advertised or stated rates have been far different from what I've experienced.

Paper Gains

You may have heard a friend or overheard someone in a crowd tell everyone about their trip to Las Vegas and how they hit the $16,000 jackpot. It was awesome!

Everybody is just fascinated and wishes they had been there to experience the thrill, right? Sure, it is exciting. No wonder they are building casinos all over the country, so more and more people can experience the same high, so to speak.

Many of you have experienced those same highs when you opened up your quarterly investment statements. We've already shown you how they calculate those numbers, but what I hope you get out of this discussion is the fact that you had no gain or loss at all, because you didn't cash out at the time you received the statement. We call those "paper gains," because those gains are worth no more than the paper they were printed on, unless you call up your stockbroker or financial adviser and have them move that money out and realize those gains. In all actuality, those probably were not truly gains if you consider that the market hasn't even recovered the losses sustained in 2008.

Do you ever wonder why they send you a statement showing you how much money is in your IRA or 401(k)? If you can't take it out without penalties until you're fifty-nine and a half anyway, does it matter how much is in there when you're thirty-five? It may be worth less at age fifty-nine and a half than it is worth now, so why bother?

The same goes for real estate, or precious metals, or wherever the flavor-of-the-week "jackpot" happens to be that quarter. We all remember when everyone supposedly had double or triple the price they had paid for their home and couldn't find a contractor to build new wings onto their homes because they were all busy building second and third homes next to the ski resort for their neighbors ... paper gains.

There are companies spending fortunes advertising gold and silver as the next "jackpot" just waiting to be taken by the highest bidder. Even though you may have those shiny little coins locked up in your safe in the basement, the metal is only worth the price on the paper advertising the latest bid price.

Lesson #1: What I was taught to be true about our investment statements, our gold bricks, or our houses has turned out not to be true, because when you hear that someone, somewhere, somehow sold their house for that unbelievable price, that must mean yours is worth that much as well. You may also find out that when you decide it is time to cash out, your gold or your 401(k) has very little value, and by the way, the gains have not yet been taxed. That never shows up on the statements either.

The only time any of these paper gains are true gains is when you cash them out. This is why you need to be sure that the money you are able to save during your working career is put into an account that will grow consistently and not be affected by these cycles in the various markets.

Lesson #2: What I was taught to be true about paper gains that has turned out not to be true is that paper gains have no purchasing power at all. They lead to a false sense of security, as lifestyle purchases are based on the paper gain, not the actual economic value of the realizable gains. During the stock market boom of the 1980s and 1990s, many people transferred safe funds to the market to participate in these gains. Consumer purchases were made along the way without a responsible transfer of the paper gains back to safe money, only to see the paper gains disappear in the early 2000s and again in 2008. If you are going to participate in the market's paper gains, you must systematically and responsibly make the paper gains into realized gains.

Your goal should be to grow your career and build liquidity as soon as possible, so you don't have to worry so much about economic downturns. More importantly, you need to be sure that on the day you decide to retire, the money you have accumulated is in a cash account that is outpacing inflation and is truly worth the number printed on that piece of paper.

Be a Long-Term Investor

A second cousin to the average-rate-of-return rule that CPAs learn is the long term investment rule. If you are a long-term investor, you can ignore the day-to-day volatility of the market. Stock market history shows that the market has a long-term upward slope of increasing returns. We are often pointed to the mountain charts discussed in the previous chapter.

The history of the S&P 500 proves this well. Just look at the following long-term average rates of return:

1942–2011	12.72	a seventy-year average
1952–2011	11.87	
1962–2011	10.66	
1972–2011	11.39	
1982–2011	12.42	
1992–2011	9.59	
2002–2012	5.03	

(*Source:* www.standardandpoors.com)

So, as long as you are looking at a time span of around twenty years or more, you will eventually get an average 11–12% on your money. Reducing these averages—because average is not what you get, but instead actual year-to-year returns—you can still amass a small fortune in the long term as long as you pay the taxes from your lifestyle.

However, these are not the returns that the average investor receives. The 2011 Dalbar Study of Investor Returns found that over the last twenty years, when the S&P 500 returned an average of 9.14%, the average equity investor earned just 3.83%. The 2012 Dalbar Study revealed that in 2011 alone, the average investor lost 573% while the S&P 500 gained 2.12% (*Source*: www.dalbar.com.)

Why is that? Part of it is investment selection, but most of the difference is allocated to investor behavior. Investors just don't buy and hold for the long term. They tend to get in the market near its high, because as the market is going up, it seems safe. Part of it is also that they don't want to be left out of the party, so they join their friends and invest. Alan Greenspan, a former Federal Reserve chairman, has referred to this as "irrational exuberance." Then, when the market corrects, they exercise some control and stay in, understanding that they are long-term investors. When they begin to see others get out of the market, they start to lose sleep, and they sell near the bottom of the correction. Then, as the market begins to recover, they wait, they vow they aren't going to be caught by a "sucker's rally," wait a little more, make sure the market is really back on the upward climb, and then get back in. They literally buy high and sell low! The human psyche is just more fragile than the computer models that can calculate the long-term rates of return we all ought to be getting if we are just patient.

Notice also that the long term is a long time. The money has to be in the market to get these returns. You can't chicken out and you can't spend the money – not even for taxes.

Lesson #1: What I was taught to be true about being a long-term investor that has turned out not to be true is that being a long-term investor requires a discipline or stubbornness that human behavior patterns rarely allow.

My oldest daughter, a graduate of one of the most highly rated public universities in America, started her career in finance a few years ago. She started her career just in time to see the stock market fall by 40% and then quickly rebound by 50%. She called on the phone and told me that she had a training presentation to give and she just couldn't get the numbers to work out; would I help her? She explained that she wanted to show how well the market had recovered from its recent collapse. She used the example of $100,000 invested in this volatile 40%-down-and-50%-up market. She quickly discovered that what she was taught to be true turned out not to be. Rates of return are not additive. And even though the premise of the previous chapter on averages would lead you to believe that over the two years you had earned 10% total, 5% average, it wasn't just untrue; it wasn't even close.

$100,000

less 40%   the market "correction"

=$60,000

plus 50%   the market "recovery"

=$90,000

I confirmed with her that her numbers were right, and instead of earning an average 5% over the two-year period, she actually lost an average 5% per year.

Then she made a remarkable statement that led to this chapter. She said, "Just think if you didn't lose money. If the 40% loss could have just been a break-even year, and then even if I just earned half of what the market earned the next year, I'd have $125,000."

Let's see how our long-term rates of return would have fared if we could eliminate all of the negatives, replace them with zeros, and take just 75% of the positives. For each of the following time periods below, you would have the stated rate of return over and above what staying in the market for the long term would have yielded.

1932–2011	36%	In other words, you would have 36% more money if you eliminated the negatives and replaced the positives with 75% of the actual return.
1942–2011	7%	
1952–2011	64%	
1962–2011	64%	
1972–2011	86%	
1982–2011	24%	
1992–2011	92%	
2002–2011	26%	

(*Source:* www.standardandpoors.com)

Here is another way to look at this. If you invested $10,000 at the beginning of each of these periods, by eliminating the negatives of the stock market but only taking 75% of the gain when the market went up, your investment nest egg would be higher in every time period.

	All the return	Eliminating the losses	More money	% More
1932–2011	33,106,148	44,890,964	11,784,816	36
1942–2011	14,498,955	15,469,919	970,964	7
1952–2011	3,174,955	5,201,750	2,026,795	64
1962–2011	901,392	1,481,962	580,570	64
1972–2011	352,102	654,356	302,253	86
1982–2011	186,498	231,745	45,247	24
1992–2011	41,818	80,113	38,295	92
2002–2011	17,115	21,501	4,386	26

This table illustrates that small advantages can mean a lot of money in real terms. For instance, the advantage of limiting the gains to only 75% in exchange for eliminating all the losses is only a 7% difference in the time period 1942–2011, which doesn't sound like much. But that is a real dollar advantage of over $970,000.

For the longest time period, 1931–2010, you would have needed to exchange the negatives for only two-thirds of the positives to break even. But remember, human behavior may have caused the investor to deviate from being a long-term investor, or he may have spent some of the money.

Lesson #2: What I was taught to be true about being a long-term investor has turned out not to be true, because taking the losses with the gains is a losing strategy. Limit your losses, even at the expense of some of your gains.

One of the longest-standing traditional investment strategies is *dollar cost averaging*; that is, getting into the market a little at a time. If you invest the same amount of money as the market is going up, your invested total grows as you add money, and you merely purchase fewer, more valuable individual shares. However, you limit your upside potential, since you didn't buy all at once at the low price. But at the same time, you are protecting your available investment dollars should the market move down unexpectedly.

If the market heads lower, you still invest the same amount of money, but you buy more shares at a lower price. You are never buying all of your position either high or low. Dollar cost averaging helps your discipline to stay in the declining market, because you are systematically buying more less-expensive shares. You continue to buy and to stay in. It seems to me that if I just don't lose money in the market, as illustrated earlier, in exchange for part of the upside, I'll sleep better at night.

Rarely is it spoken of to "dollar cost average" out of the market. If you take a look at the ten years, 1999–2008, you find that you would have been better off taking principal out during the downturn (limiting your loss of principal) and taking gains out during the upturn (protecting what the market gave you). Here is a simple example of removing 5% of your initial investment over this ten-year period of time.

This first chart shows the results had you left the money in the market over the entire period of time. (*Source:* www.standardandpoors.com.) An initial investment of $100,000 would have been worth $73,461 ten years later.

	Rate of return	Beginning of the year	Gain/loss	End of the year
1999	19.51%	100,000	19,510	119,510
2000	-10.14%	119,510	-12,118	107,392
2001	-13.04%	107,392	-14,004	93,388
2002	-23.37%	93,388	-21,825	71,563
2003	26.38%	71,563	18,878	90,441
2004	8.99%	90,441	8,131	98,572
2005	3.00%	98,572	2,957	101,529
2006	13.62%	101,529	13,828	115,358
2007	3.53%	115,358	4,072	119,430
2008	-38.49%	119,430	-45,968	73,461

What if you had exercised the strategy of dollar cost averaging yourself out of the market, as outlined above, and removed 5% of the original investment ($5,000) each year? The growth chart would look like this:

	Withdrawal	Rate of return	Beginning of the year	Gain/loss	End of the year
1999	-5,000	19.51%	95,000	18,535	113,535
2000	-5,000	-10.14%	108,535	-11,005	97,529
2001	-5,000	-13.04%	92,529	-12,066	80,463
2002	-5,000	-23.37%	75,463	-17,636	57,828
2003	-5,000	26.38%	52,828	13,936	66,763
2004	-5,000	8.99%	61,763	5,553	67,316
2005	-5,000	3.00%	62,316	1,869	64,185
2006	-5,000	13.62%	59,185	8,061	67,247
2007	-5,000	3.53%	62,247	2,197	64,444
2008	-5,000	-38.49%	59,444	-22,880	36,564

By stripping off a percentage of the account each year, you would end up with $36,564 plus the $50,000 you stripped off, resulting in a total of $86,564. If you had just left the money in the account because you are a long-term investor, you would have $73,461, a difference of $13,103. This difference assumes you stuck the $5,000 into a mattress for safekeeping. Perhaps the money ought to land in an account that can be safe, secure, and tax-free to avoid the pitfalls of traditional CPA thinking that we have already discovered.

Lesson #3: What I was taught to be true about being a long-term investor has turned out not to be true, because leaving all of your eggs in one basket, taking the downs with the ups, may not be any better than systematically removing risk from your investments by retreating to tax-free safety.

Qualified Plans

A qualified plan is any arrangement in which the government provides a tax deduction for making an investment and allows the growth in the account to be tax deferred. A qualified plan is commonly known as a 401(k), 403(b), 457, or SEP plan. Not only do you get the miracle of compound interest working in your favor, but also you don't have to pay the tax—until you take the money out of the plan.

All of these plans are provided by your employer and offer a vast but limited array of investment choices, anywhere from aggressive growth funds to stable value funds. The funds allowed for investment by your employer must include investment choices spread out over the spectrum of risk; however, you are not required to put a set amount in any one fund. The money you put into one of these employer plans is always yours, but sometimes you must meet certain criteria to actually access your money. Some of those requirements may include attaining a certain age, terminating your employment, or suffering a government-defined hardship.

Some employers sweeten the pot for you to participate. The enticement sounds like this: "If you put your money in, we (the employer) will put some in as well." The amount put in by the employer is defined by the employer, subject to government-mandated testing for discrimination against the lower-paid employees, and it may be subject to certain criteria. Some of these requirements include working a certain number of hours minimum each year or being employed on the last day of the year. Most of the time, employer contributions are subject to a vesting schedule; if you don't stay employed, all or a portion of the employer contributions made to your account is forfeited. The money the employer puts into the plan is tax-deductible for the employer, much like general compensation is, and is allowed to grow tax-deferred. Because the employer receives a tax deduction and the money in the account grows tax-deferred, all of the money is taxable to the employee when it is withdrawn.

An IRA is an individual retirement account that you can set up for yourself if you are not a member of an employer-qualified plan. You get a tax deduction for the money you put in, and it grows tax-deferred. There are methods to consolidate IRA accounts with employer-qualified plans where the employer money is made available to you through a process called a trustee-to-trustee transfer or rollover. Investment opportunities available in an IRA are virtually limitless.

What makes these arrangements so attractive is that ...

1. You don't have to pay current income taxes on the money as it goes in, nor do you have to pay current income taxes on the growth of the money each year.

2. You are investing by "dollar cost averaging," buying more shares when the price of the investment is low and buying fewer shares when the price is high, consequently averaging out the cost of participating in the plan.

3. You are taking advantage of the miracle of compound interest. Because this is a retirement plan, it is based on a lifetime of working, theoretically thirty years or

more. From a previous chapter, we've learned that it takes time for the miracle to take shape, so it has a real possibility to work in this situation.

4. Your investment is being made as a payroll deduction; therefore, you hardly notice the money is gone. What you don't see, you don't spend, and you are saving for your retirement systematically.

We are taught to save for retirement systematically, because a little sacrifice now will provide a great benefit later. If you can get your employer to kick in some money, that is like getting a free rate of return. Because it grows tax-deferred (although it is sometimes described as tax-free), it becomes a powerful retirement savings tool. A qualified plan is one of the most explosive accumulation tools available to most employees.

It is hard to argue with all of these benefits. However, it is these very advantages that contribute to making these plans erosive to your wealth when you need it the most: in your retirement years. When you begin to peel back the layers, like an onion, it begins to smell! You discover that what we have been taught to be true isn't true at all and may be one of the worst hoaxes ever perpetrated on the American worker.

Let's see what I was taught to be true about qualified plans and that I have discovered, over years of practical experience, isn't true.

First, I was taught that we are saving taxes by putting money into a qualified plan.

If you were to go to the bank and ask the banker for a loan, and he said your loan was approved, what two questions would you want an answer to before you accepted the money? You would want to know what interest rate the bank was going to charge and when the bank wanted the money back. What if the banker told you that at the present time, the bank had plenty of money and didn't need the money back right away? In fact, you could keep the money until the bank needed it, and at that point it would determine the interest rate. Would you take the bank's money? Of course not!

That bank loan example is similar to what we are doing when we participate in a tax-deferred qualified plan. The IRS is due the income taxes on the income we earn, with a few exceptions. One of the exceptions is money we put into a qualified plan. The taxes that would otherwise be due on the money we put into the qualified plan are deferred until some uncertain time. For the most part, we are in charge of when we pay these taxes, as we use the qualified plan money as income in retirement, but the IRS demands that we begin paying the taxes at age seventy and a half. Could the IRS change the required minimum distribution age? Sure they could. The taxes we defer are similar to taking a loan from the IRS for money that the IRS is otherwise due today, and agreeing to pay it back according to the IRS's schedule and at the income tax rate in effect at that time. Could the IRS forgive the tax "loan"? Sure it could. Could the IRS assess a tax rate higher or lower than the tax rate that was in effect when the taxes were deferred? Sure it could. Could the IRS assess a "success" tax on qualified plan balances over a certain amount that it might believe to be excessive? Sure it could. Which do you think is a more likely outcome? Tax forgiveness? A higher future tax rate? An excise tax? When we participate in a qualified plan, we are agreeing to pay these taxes otherwise due today, at some uncertain date, at some uncertain rate. Would you agree to that with your banker?

Lesson #1: What I was taught to be true about qualified plans has turned out not to be true, because qualified plans do not save taxes. They merely defer the tax to some uncertain date, at some uncertain rate. Qualified plans do not avoid income taxes; they merely put them off until later.

Okay, so we defer the tax; what is the big deal? It is just a word. "If I put $5,000 into a deductible IRA, and I'm in the 25% tax bracket, I save—I mean defer—$1,250. I will just pay it later, because I can earn interest on the $1,250 I don't pay today." Let's think about that.

If this were your plan for thirty years, you would have put aside $150,000, and you would have deferred $37,500 of income taxes. If that account were invested and received an average 8% return each year, your retirement account would be worth $611,729. If you chose to supplement your other retirement income with this money for twenty years in retirement, at 8% you could withdraw $54,338 per year before you would run out of money. See what I mean about being taught that this is one of the most explosive accumulation tools of all time? If you started paying the $1,250 taxes deferred each year when you were adding money to the account, you would net out $53,088. "Big deal!" you say. "That is still a large sum of money to supplement my other retirement income."

But it doesn't work that way! You don't just pay back what you deferred; you pay back an amount equal to the tax rate in the year you withdraw it, and assessed against the entire amount you withdraw. If you are still in the 25% tax bracket (which way do you think taxes are headed in the future?), your annual tax bill will be $13,597 each year for twenty years. That is $271,940 in taxes paid during your withdrawal years. So much for saving taxes! In fact, the taxes saved, $37,500, are paid in less than three years of retirement. Even though you have paid the government all of the taxes deferred from your contributions, you get to keep paying them to cover all of the taxes deferred on what your investment earned, until your qualified plan account is exhausted.

To add insult to injury, if you withdraw an amount in excess of a government-mandated amount, your withdrawal will subject your Social Security payments to income taxes. If you can stay under the amount that the government says you can have, your Social Security will be tax-free. It makes you wonder who owns these accounts!

Some choose to leave the money in the qualified plan and not use it. You can't do that either! The government wants its money! Beginning at age seventy and a half, you are told—no, you are supposed to know—the amount you have to take out each year. If you don't get it right, then the government will tell you what you should have taken out, and will access the income tax due on what you should have taken out, and add as a penalty 50% of what should have been taken out. That doesn't leave much for you!

Some choose to take out only what they have to and leave the rest for the kids at their death. That doesn't work either; your children get to pay the tax. Uncle Sam always gets its money. When we leave a qualified plan as an inheritance, we not only leave the account value as an inheritance but also a tax bill. Thanks, Mom and Dad!

Lesson #2: What I was taught to be true about qualified plans has turned out not to be true, because while some describe these arrangements as tax-free because you don't pay the current income taxes on the amount put into the plan, they are far from tax-free. As your account compounds, so do your income taxes.

Another lesson in the above example is that not only do qualified plans defer the tax, but they also defer the tax calculation. The tax rate you would have paid had you not participated in the qualified plan may or may not be the rate at which you will pay your taxes when the taxes are due. Ask yourself, "Do I think tax rates are going to go up in the future, go down in the future, or stay the same?" Consider that Social Security is going broke, Medicare needs to be fixed, and the Pension Benefit Guaranty Corporation is out of money. Not only is there pressure for general income tax brackets to go up, but your personal income tax rate goes up as well, because most likely ...

- you have paid off your home mortgage, consequently losing the tax deduction associated with home mortgage interest;

- your children have exceeded the age at which you receive a child tax credit; and

- by the time you are retired, your children are no longer dependents and are no longer qualified for personal exemptions on your tax return.

Lesson #3: What I was taught to be true about qualified plans has turned out not to be true, because qualified plans not only defer the taxes, but they also defer the tax calculation. You will pay taxes at whatever the tax rate is at the time you have to pay the tax.

We were also taught that you will retire in a lower tax bracket than when you were working. That might be true if you are saving for retirement truly tax-free, but, as discussed, these qualified plans are anything but tax-free. If all of your retirement income will come from a tax-deferred source like a qualified plan, a successful retirement means that you are merely trading your taxable paycheck for a taxable IRA distribution.

Another principle we were taught was that you can retire on 70% of your pre-retirement income.

Lessons #4 and #5: What I was taught to be true about qualified plans has turned out not to be true, because you most probably will not retire in a lower tax bracket, and I have yet to see anyone able to live on 70% of what they can't live on today anyway. To be comfortable in retirement, you have to have complete replacement of your pre-retirement income, or we will need to build a lot more Walmarts so we can create more greeter jobs.

The last lesson about qualified plans we are going to talk about is ownership. Just because your name is on your quarterly plan statement doesn't mean that the money is yours. First, you have to meet the vesting requirements of your employer to claim ownership of the employer's matching contributions. Even after that, the account is not yours. Because of the uncertainties of taxation, the government has first claim on your account. After the taxes are paid, at whatever the rate is in the future, the rest is finally yours. Could the government raise the tax rate in the future? Could it raise the tax on just qualified plans to something greater than the normal tax rate? Could it reinstate the old excess withdrawal tax, or institute a windfall elimination tax on qualified plans? I'll leave the answer to you, but why chance it?

Lesson #6: What I was taught to be true about qualified plans has turned out not to be true, because the government has the first claim on the distributions from my qualified plan; I get the portion the government doesn't take away in taxes first.

Qualified plans may be the most efficient method of accumulating money for retirement, but they can be the most inefficient when you need the money the most.

Buy Term and Invest the Rest

Life insurance is often considered a necessary evil: something you pay for and never receive anything for it. Life insurance is designed to help a family financially if the income earner meets with an early demise. The question you have to ask yourself is what would your spouse and your children do if you were to die? In this sense, life insurance ought to be labeled death insurance.

Some might say, "My spouse will remarry"; others will say, "He (or she) will get a job, or a second job." Others will say, "If I buy enough life insurance, he (or she) will not have to do either. My family will move ahead without me or a financial hardship."

Before I address the "buy term and invest the rest" response, let me address these first two solutions.

If you say your spouse will remarry, have you ever had that conversation before it became your conclusion? If not, I'd suggest you do. If your spouse remarried, what would you want for him or her? Would you like the second marriage to be for love or for money? It sure is a lot easier when financial concerns can be removed from the remarriage question and the answer can come from the same perspective in which you married—for love!

Lesson #1: I was taught that I didn't need life insurance, and that has turned out not to be true, because if it is ever my spouse's desire to remarry after my death, I want it to be out of love, not because of the need for money.

If you say your spouse will get a job, have you ever considered why your spouse isn't working now? If it is for the consideration of child-rearing, does the dream of Mom or Dad staying home with kids change just because someone has died? I would think not. During the period of dating and engagement, many dreams are constructed. After marriage, these dreams are begun and carried out over a lifetime. Life insurance is the only thing that can ensure that the dreams of our early years really do come true. So life insurance isn't really a necessary evil—life insurance is a dream realizer. The necessary evil is paying for it. Traditional CPA training says to "buy term and invest the rest"; it is the least costly way to go.

Lesson #2: What I was taught to be true about not needing life insurance has turned out not to be true, because if my spouse ever has to face the future without me (or my income), I don't want it to have to change all of the hopes and dreams we had together. I don't want her to have to work if she doesn't want to. I still want my children to go to the college of their choice and not settle for something more affordable that doesn't offer the curriculum that they would like to pursue, or not attain a college degree at all.

Before we can calculate the cost of life insurance, we must first calculate how much death benefit is necessary. Consider a wage earner earning $100,000 a year. This is a good amount to consider, because it is easily scalable; if you earn $200,000, just double the calculations, and so on. If a spouse needed to replace $100,000 per year, and he or she could earn 5% consistently and safely, a nest egg of $2,000,000 would be necessary. Some would consider this nest egg the deceased's human life value, but it falls short when you account for what the future may hold. All this amount means is that the family could continue to live at the same standard without the need to generate the lost wage through trading their time for money. That is twenty times income, and for many insurance companies, it stretches the upper limits of what they will provide. This ignores the likelihood of earning 5% every year and the family need for periodic lump sums for things like cars, vacations, college educations, and weddings. Add these to the mix, and the answer to the deceased person's human life value is better defined: as much as the insurance company is willing to provide.

Lesson #3: What I was taught to be true about "buy term and invest the rest" has turned out not to be true, because there is no sum of money that an insurance company will issue that can fund the hopes and desires that my family and I dreamed about.

Term life insurance can be purchased in various ways, either with an annual premium amount that increases with age, or a with a premium that stays level for a certain period of time and then increases after that with age. At a certain point the annual increases in cost are prohibitive, but that is designed to happen after the children are grown, through college, and on their own, otherwise known as "off the family payroll"! It is now that Mom and Dad in their retirement years no longer feel the "need" for life insurance; therefore, when it gets too expensive, they just drop the policy and consider themselves "self-insured." They become "self-insured" because during that same time period, they accumulate a nest egg equal to the amount of term life insurance that just expired. These two premises are the hallmarks of the "buy term and invest the rest" rule.

Let's consider a hypothetical twenty-five-year-old, just married and starting a family, earning $100,000 per year. The hypothetical premium for a $2,000,000 life insurance contract whose premium is level for ten years, with the buyer in the best of health, and with no bells and whistles for "convertibility" or "premium waivers for disability," is $385 per year for ten years. Pretty cheap!

Let's stop right there, because I was taught that when purchasing life insurance, you should pay as little as possible; don't purchase all of those extra riders. There is a lesson here.

The rider for "convertibility" is a provision that allows you to convert your term policy within a specified period of time, for an amount equal to the amount of the term policy, to a permanent life insurance policy, without having to have your health rescreened for pricing and issuance purposes. Of course, if you are buying term and investing the difference, why would you ever consider anything other than another term policy?

Consider a few scenarios.

Scenario 1: You are at the end of the level portion of your term policy. The $385 is about to go up to $4,445 in year eleven, and during the last ten years you have started to smoke. Your alternative here is to take another term policy, but no longer at the best insurance rates; once the insurance company realizes you picked up the habit of smoking during the last ten years, the new ten-year term policy is no longer $385 a year, but now $4,085. This is still not $4,445, but it is fairly discouraging. You choose this new policy, but you don't have much of the "invest the rest" money left. Additionally, after another ten years, you have the same decision to make, and to continue this new term policy will now cost $18,365!

Scenario 2: Your life has gone according to plan; however, toward the conclusion of your last term policy at age sixty-four, you are diagnosed with terminal cancer, and you aren't expected to live more than another five years. You can keep the original plan in place and surrender the term policy. After coming to terms with your shortened life expectancy, you realize that there is now a significant investment opportunity for your family, offering a better rate of return than you ever experienced in your "invest the rest," by keeping your term policy. If you keep this last term policy, having paid $5,985 for each of the last ten years, the cost to continue the policy in year eleven is $61,965, but for a redemption value of $2,000,000 (a 3,000% rate of return), it is a good investment. If you live past the eleventh year, the twelfth-year premium is $68,125: still a two-year rate of return of 1,400%. If you live twice the number of years your doctor first estimated (ten more years), your rate of return is still more than 10% per year on average. The return might be great, but the problem it presents is complex.

- First, each year you have to reconsider your diagnosis and your mortality, even though you are "beating it."

- Second, you will need to pump over $970,000 into the term life insurance policy, and you might live longer than another ten years.

- If, at any point after paying that eleventh-year premium, you stop funding the life insurance policy, it makes the previous year's decision to pay the premium a poor decision.

- As you pay the premiums each year, and you live off of your "invest the rest" nest egg, what is the status of your nest egg?

If the original term policy had the term-to-permanent insurance conversion rider, the smoking decision and the cancer diagnosis would not have been an issue. The rider would have provided alternatives that weren't available if this rider was not purchased in the original term insurance policy.

Lesson #4: What I was taught to be true about "buy term and invest the rest" has turned out not to be true, because there is both economic and emotional value in the convertibility rider of a life insurance policy. The economic value comes from being able to keep the level of death benefit for a set future cost that will never change despite health changes. The emotional value is in not having to revisit my mortality each year should I ever have to "beat" a disease. The consideration each year of paying another enormous premium alone could be hazardous to my health.

The other rider that I was taught to avoid when buying term and investing the rest was the rider that would waive the premium for the life insurance should I ever become disabled. Studies by the Social Security Administration demonstrate that a twenty-year-old worker has a 30% chance of becoming disabled before he or she reaches retirement age. (*Source:* www.ltdrates.com.) A forty-year-old male is twice as likely to become disabled before age sixty five than he is to die. (*Source:* http://www.protectyourincome.com/education-center/disability-facts-and-statistics/probability.) Given the previous example regarding the convertibility lesson, for that same person who unexpectedly was diagnosed with cancer, the disability waiver would eliminate the continual "investment" of future premiums until the eventual $2,000,000 payoff at death. Now that is a rate of return we can't even calculate!

Lesson #5: What I was taught to be true about "buy term and invest the rest" has turned out not to be true, because there is also economic and emotional value in the disability waiver of premium rider of a life insurance policy. The economic value comes from not having to make continual premium payments during years of lower income because of disability. The emotional value is having the peace of mind that when the eventual death occurs, the hopes of future dreams will still live on without the additional monetary outlays.

Back to the hallmark of "buy term and invest the rest": buy enough temporary "death" insurance to replace the wage earner's income, and invest what you would have otherwise spent on permanent life insurance.

Remember that the recommended minimum insurance for a twenty-five-year-old, $100,000 income earner is $2,000,000, and that amount of temporary term insurance costs $385 per year for the first ten years.

At this individual's age thirty-five, the premium on this policy goes to $4,445—not too cheap anymore—so he goes shopping for another ten-year level-term policy. This time, his health has slipped a bit—a little cholesterol problem, that's all—and his $2,000,000 policy premium becomes $585, which is still considered cheap. But we begin to have a problem: $585 no longer covers his human life value any longer, because in those ten years between ages twenty-five and thirty-five, he has gotten a raise and is now earning $150,000. Now his human life value is $3,000,000, and the premium goes to $835. If you are thinking, "They don't really need that much," all I can say is shame on you. If this were you, what are you willing to cut out of your family (age thirty-five) lifestyle, which now includes not only your spouse, but also three children, ages eight, five, and two?

You are now forty-five years of age, you have one child entering college and two in high school, your income is now $200,000, and your term premium in year eleven is $14,065. Whoa—let's apply for another ten-year policy. The insurance company has now started to lower its multiple on you. Instead of providing twenty times your income, the company will provide only fifteen times your income; after all, you were supposed to be "investing the rest." So the company will provide the same $3,000,000 at one more reduced health rating, because you've become "too short" for the same health rating as before, meaning that your height hasn't kept up with your weight changes, and your new ten-year premium would be $2,875 per year. Ouch, from $835 to $2,875, with your oldest child just entering college and two not far behind!

Now you are fifty-five, and you figure you must work to sixty-five because you have to replace all of that tuition you spent from the "invest the rest" pile; so you have one more ten-year time frame to cover. Reducing the multiplier to ten times your income, assuming you have topped off at $200,000 per year, your last ten-year policy is at standard rates, since you now have added some negative family history to your personal health record, and you find yourself spending $6,255 per year.

It is now the night before your official retirement dinner, and you are alone with your spouse at your favorite restaurant; you look lovingly into your spouse's eyes, and you begin to reminisce about all of those years of working and raising a family. You tell her that the plan has worked, that all of those years of paying for all of that cheap term insurance has finally come to an end, and that tomorrow you are going to cancel your policy. Today, she would get $2,000,000, but tomorrow, because your plan was so successful, she will get $0. Hope you make it through the night!

Let's add up all of that cheap insurance. The $385 per year for the first ten years is $3,850, $835 per year for the second ten years is $8,350, $2,875 per year for the third ten is $28,750, and $6,255 for each of the last ten years is $62,550, for a grand total of $103,500. But that is only part of the cost. What you are not counting is what you otherwise could have earned on that money had you not spent it. This is known as *opportunity cost*. Every dollar spent is a dollar that can never be saved or spent again, and neither can it earn what it might have earned while in your possession. If we put the flows of money for what the term insurance cost over those forty years in an account earning 6% (your "invest the rest" experience), you discover that the true cost of that insurance was $227,638. Assuming you made it through the night after you disclosed to your spouse that you were dropping the insurance policy, the next question you must answer is whether this amount you have put in trust with the insurance company is going to be refunded to you, since they never had to pay out the death benefit. The answer is no; this money is not going to be available for your use in retirement.

Assuming you live to life expectancy, another twenty years, that amount of money the life insurance company didn't refund continued to grow at the life insurance company at 6%. Your $227,638 has now become $730,067; surely that will be refunded to your children now that you have passed on. No. In fact, the insurance company continues to keep it, and keeps it another twenty years, to the point at which you would have been one hundred years of age. The insurance company has the tidy sum of $1,749,649, an amount of money that almost equals your initial death benefit when you were twenty-five years old, and an amount of money that certainly would have served both you and your children well in all of your retirement years. All of this assumes that you succeeded at your "buy term and invest the rest" objective—you didn't die before retirement.

Lesson #6: I was taught to buy term insurance and invest the rest, and that has turned out not to be true, because term insurance is not the least expensive way to buy life insurance. It is a very expensive way to buy life insurance, when you account for all of the costs.

Human nature plays a role in this age-old approach. The complement to "buy term" is "invest the rest." If you don't invest the rest, this plan doesn't work; in fact, it fails miserably! All of the emotional factors noted in previous chapters come into play here, and usually somewhere along the way, "invest the rest" is abandoned; whatever was invested is spent for things like vacation and college educations. The reality of "invest the rest" is that it doesn't happen.

Lesson #7: What I was taught to be true about "buy term insurance and invest the rest" has turned out not to be true, because few people invest the rest.

As disclosed in the "Rate of Return" and "Be a Long-Term Investor" chapters, the rates of return advertised in the marketplace just aren't what the individual investor realizes. Let's look at the trend of long-term interest rates over the last twenty years:

S&P 500 Total Return

	Average Rate of Return	Actual Rate of Return
1992–2011	9.59%	7.81%
1993–2011	9.70%	7.82%
1994–2011	9.67%	7.70%
1995–2011	10.17%	8.09%
1996–2011	8.45%	6.48%
1997–2011	7.49%	5.46%
1998–2011	5.64%	3.69%
1999–2011	3.87%	1.98%
2000–2011	2.44%	0.57%
2001–2011	3.49%	1.44%
2002–2011	5.03%	2.89%
2003–2011	8.04%	6.14%
2004–2011	5.46%	3.63%
2005–2011	4.69%	2.64%
2006–2011	4.65%	2.21%
2007–2011	2.42%	-0.20%
2008–2011	1.66%	-1.53%
2009–2011	14.54%	12.33%
2010-2011	8.59%	8.17%

(*Source:* www.standardandpoors.com)

Remember, because your actual experience in the market is year-to-year, you do not earn the average rate of return; you actually earn something less. Not only do you earn something less than the average that is advertised, but you must also pay investment fees from that and income taxes on the growth, assuming that you did your investing outside of your employer 401(k) or 403(b) plan or personal traditional IRA. If you did your investing in any of these plans, the taxes you owe will apply on all of the account balance, at whatever the tax rate is at the time you begin to withdraw the money from the account.

The eventual withdrawals from your permanent life insurance contract, if withdrawn properly, with the expert help of your life insurance agent, will come to you without a tax. In fact, it will be sent to you in a way that is not even reportable to the Internal Revenue Service by either you or your life insurance company.

The benefits of proper withdrawals from a life insurance contract have a snowball effect. Because these distributions are not reportable on your tax return, they are not considered when determining whether your social security payments are taxable. If your only additional income in retirement is from your permanent life insurance contract, your social security will also be tax-free. If, instead, your additional cash flow in retirement comes from a qualified plan such as a 401(k), 403(b), or IRA, that cash flow is accounted for when determining the taxability of your social security payments, resulting in up to 85% of your social security payments being subject to income tax at whatever the tax rate is that year.

Lesson #8: What I was taught to be true about "buy term insurance and invest the rest" has turned out not to be true, because, as evidenced by the last twenty years, it is very difficult to beat the internal rate of return of a permanent life insurance contract after you account for fees and taxes.

Collateral Capacity

"There is something that is more powerful than all the armies in the world, and that is an idea whose time has come." —Victor Hugo

Many of the people that I work with have a large amount of cash-value permanent life insurance on themselves and on key family members, and they don't know how to use it. There will be many times during your career or in your personal life that you will need a cash cushion, and the cash value of life insurance can serve that purpose! Once in force, this will become your "private reserve" that will be available for you to collateralize major purchases such as a car, tuition, or wedding expenses. It is available to use as an emergency fund, or just to build a massive retirement fund that, if done properly, can be accessed tax-free. As it grows, you are basically building up your "collateral capacity," which will allow you to forgo traditional secured bank financing and set up your own unstructured loan (*i.e.,* no structured repayment schedule, although any outstanding loan balance will reduce the death benefit) from the life insurance company using your cash value as collateral.

When we talk about life insurance, we are not talking about just any kind of life insurance; we are talking about custom-designed cash-value permanent life insurance, funded up to *but not over* the government allowable modified endowment contract (MEC) limits, which will focus the policy on the cash-value growth within the policy. The reason we want to stay below the MEC limits is that loans and withdrawals from cash-value permanent life policies that are classified as modified endowment contracts may be subject to tax at the time that a loan or withdrawal is taken, and, if prior to age fifty-nine and a half, a 10% federal tax penalty may apply. A qualified adviser will show you how to structure the policy, and once you have the money in the policy, it will become the lifeblood of your financial portfolio, while eliminating the need for many of the other money buckets you were told you needed in the past. This one bucket will do the work of several, and it will give you liquidity, use, and control of your money.

Lesson #1: What I was taught to be true about life insurance has turned out not to be true, because life insurance is about more than just its value at death.

Another advantage of permanent life insurance is that it allows you higher contribution limits than you might have with qualified plan funds while still maintaining tax-deferred growth. With higher limits on the amount of money that can be put in, we must be sure that the policy premiums are affordable, because if they are not paid, the policy could lapse or incur surrender charges. You also want to be sure that any withdrawals or loans that you make won't cause a loss of the no-lapse guarantee, if one is provided for in the policy. If tax-free loans are taken and the policy lapses, a taxable event could occur; once again, be sure to consult with a qualified adviser to be sure that your life insurance contract is set up properly, so you are getting the full benefit of a permanent life insurance policy in the first place, which is to avoid all those taxes and penalties that you have with qualified plans.

Lesson #2: What I was taught to be true about life insurance has turned out not to be true, because life insurance is not a commodity; it is a unique tool that, when structured properly, can be one of the most valuable assets you can own.

Once this pool of money is properly established and structured properly, it will never drop in value and will continue to grow uninterrupted during a recession or even a depression. Policy guarantees are based on the financial strength and claims-paying ability of the insurance company that issues the policy, and the money can be used for any expense you incur, or for any opportunity that may present itself.

Lesson #3: What I was taught to be true about life insurance has turned out not to be true, because life insurance, during my lifetime, is about the "living benefits" and not only the death benefits. I was never taught about the "living benefits"; I always thought I had to die.

I've already shown you the advantages you will have once this reserve is established, but I am going to oversimplify it, just in order to show clearly how it would work.

Remember back when you were eight years old and started your first paper route? You probably only made about $22 per month, so it took quite some time to save any money. Your goal was to eventually save $100 so you could buy an incredible Schwinn ten-speed, metallic-brown bike that you would go and look at each week in the bicycle shop. It probably took about six months' pay to finally have enough in your savings to purchase the bike. What a great day it was going to be, and you may still remember it as if it were yesterday. So you walked down to the bank and asked the teller to give you all the money in your account. The teller gave you the $100, you put it in your pocket, and you went straight to the bike shop. It was absolutely one of the best days of your life, and the bike was worth every penny of that $100!

The reason I tell you this story is that on the surface, everything worked out, and you got good use out of your money, as this was your vehicle of choice for the next ten years while delivering papers, getting to school, having fun with friends, and so on. But if we look a little closer, we will realize that you no longer had any money in your savings and that just as you were building enough to see your interest begin to grow, you were back to $0. You would have to work for several more months just to get back where you started.

Every purchase we make is really a decision to finance the purchase. We think that we only finance a purchase when we purchase something by borrowing money. Even if we pay cash, the cash we pay is no longer in the account where it was earning interest or dividends. In fact, we are borrowing from our own futures. The lost earnings represent the financing cost of the transaction.

Imagine if that $100 were still in your account and growing with interest while you had the use of the bike. At a 5% interest rate, that $100 would have grown to $776.16 by age fifty! If your money is in a permanent life insurance contract, once the cash value in your policy has been established, you have the collateral capacity to structure your purchase in a way that benefits you the most. This simple bicycle illustration can be expanded to anything you purchase, and you can apply this same principle to your full advantage.

Lesson #4: What I was taught to be true about life insurance has turned out not to be true, because a permanent life insurance contract is not just a one-dimensional financial product. The cash value within your permanent life insurance will grow and build collateral capacity, so that other compounding interest accounts will not be diminished every time you make a purchase.

Lesson #5: I was taught that you don't really need life insurance past retirement age, because by then you will be "self-insured." "Self-insured" merely means you have accumulated sufficient assets that you no longer believe you need life insurance. This is merely another way of teaching that life insurance is just a one-dimensional financial product. At retirement your permanent life insurance contract may unlock the true value of your other assets, as they are consumed to sustain your retirement lifestyle.

If anyone tells you that you do not need life insurance, ask them if they will provide a succession plan for your family. Ask them if they will provide the money your spouse and children will need to pay the bills that do not go away at your death. If you have a permanent life insurance policy equal to the value of your retirement assets, you will be able to consume your assets, not merely live on what interest they can pay, because you know that the value of your death benefits will someday replenish all the money you spent during retirement.

Permanent life insurance is the only way to assure that what you want to happen will happen. It takes the guesswork out of saving for the future, and it takes away the uncertainty that you have when you have your money tied up in risk-based investments.

All being "self-insured" will do for you is to put you back into a situation of spending your compounding interest accounts, just as you may have done to purchase your first bicycle, stunting your true potential.

Your Home Is Your Greatest Asset

Even after the bursting of the real estate bubble, people still consider their homes to be their greatest assets.

During the last thirty years, home prices increased year after year, and that growth happened regardless of what the homeowner/investor did or didn't do, as long as he or she practiced routine maintenance of the property. The homeowner/investor, because he or she lives in the house, does not face the decision of whether to stay in the market or get out. In fact, unless forced to sell because of other unwise financing decisions, today's homeowner continues to "stay in the market" because the house represents the home rather than an investment. The homeowner is not experiencing the emotion of getting out during a down cycle, which usually means missing the market rebound. Recognizing the house as the home rather than as an investment is the proper viewpoint, rather than seeing the home as the greatest asset.

Let's look at an example to illustrate a few points.

Purchase price: $220,000

Purchase date: January 1995

Market price (2007): $380,000

Had this homeowner cashed out of the property in 2007, the rate of return for the thirteen-year period would have been 72%—a great return. However, when broken down, like we break down other returns, to an average annual rate of return, that would have been 4.3% per year. But the homeowner was focused on neither the 72% nor the 4.3%, but instead on the increase of $160,000.

Lesson #1: What I was taught to be true about my home being my best investment has turned out not to be true, because I was taught to focus on the wrong number.

There is nothing wrong with a gain of $160,000, or even 4.3% per year, especially when I consider that under current tax law, that gain and rate of return is tax-free. It rivals many of our investments available today.

But that is not the whole story; the homeowner properly had his home insured for a loss that might have been experienced through a fire, tornado, flood, earthquake, hurricane, or other peril. In the Midwest (without the threat of a hurricane), the typical cost of homeowner's insurance for a home valued like this would be $1,000 per year. This required "holding" cost of this asset brings the average rate of return down from 4.3% to 3.8%. I consider this a required holding cost because if you own your home with a mortgage associated with it, the mortgage company is going to require you to obtain a homeowner's insurance contract. If you fail to insure the property, your mortgage company will – at enormous rates! One of the pieces of paper in the stack of paper you signed at your home closing was an agreement that allows your mortgage company to buy insurance if you fail to do so.

Homeowner's insurance is not the only required holding cost. There is a little annual expenditure called real estate tax. The amount of real estate tax varies from state to state, but the real estate tax for a home as described in Illinois is about $6,000 per year. In thirteen years, this homeowner would have paid $78,000 in real estate taxes. Factoring this in as a holding cost drives the annual rate of return down to 1.55%.

Beyond the holding costs, there are maintenance costs. These are voluntary, but if you don't do them, your home appreciation will not be as described. This home was purchased when it was seven years old, so in 2007, it was a twenty-year-old home. During the course of ownership, this homeowner/investor did the following:

Updated the landscaping	$3,000
Repaired the property grading and drainage	$5,000
Replaced the roof	$10,000
Upgraded the interior decorating	$5,000
Replaced half of the windows	$3,500
Replaced the air conditioning and furnace	$5,000
TOTAL	$31,500

Accounting for these necessary maintenance costs, the annual rate of return becomes .8%—not exactly the rate of return of our "greatest asset."

Lesson #2: What I was taught to be true about my home being my best investment has turned out not to be true, because when I account for all of the costs associated with keeping the asset, the rate of return on the overall value of the house dives drastically.

Now let's consider the real estate market. In 2011, this home currently has a market value of $265,000. The current annual rate of return over the past seventeen years is a *negative* 1.5%, even though it is still worth $45,000 more than what was paid for — certainly not your greatest financial asset.

Lesson #3: I was taught that my home was a virtually riskless asset, but this has turned out not to be true.

Closely associated with home ownership is homeownership financing. Homeownership financing is where the "greatest asset" term ought to be applied; however, we are taught that a home mortgage debt is bad and that we ought to get the home paid off as soon as possible.

What is the least expensive way to purchase a home—with cash, with a fifteen-year mortgage, or with a thirty-year mortgage? Let's simplify the math and this time use a home purchased for $250,000. We also need to assume what the investor's best alternative rate of return is. Let's say the best the investor can do in the investment markets is 5%. We also need to consider the tax savings of mortgage deductibility; let's assume a marginal tax rate of 30%.

Most would assume that the least costly way to purchase the home, if you had the money, would be to pay cash. That would be an outlay of $250,000. If the purchaser pays $250,000, that means he or she doesn't have $250,000 to invest any longer. Since we are going to compare this to a fifteen- and a thirty-year mortgage, we need to pick the evaluation period as thirty years. In thirty years, invested at 5%, the $250,000 would grow to $1,080,485. So the cost to live in the home over thirty years, if the purchaser pays cash, is $1,080,485.

Comparing the two mortgages, assume the following:

Down payment: 20%	$50,000	
Amount to borrow	$200,000	

	30-year mortgage	15-year mortgage
Interest rate	6%	5.5%
Investment rate of return	5%	5%
Interest expended	$231,676	$94,150

Many people stop the analysis right there and conclude that they don't want to spend as much in interest as the home costs. Therefore, only on the basis of interest paid, they decide to pay cash (no interest). If they don't have the cash, they decide that the fifteen-year mortgage is better than the thirty-year mortgage because they will pay $137,526 less in interest.

However, just as with home appreciation, that is not the whole story. Every year, they pay mortgage interest. Because mortgage interest is potentially a tax-deductible item, you must include the tax savings that they will experience. Furthermore, the tax savings need to be brought forward to the thirty-year evaluation horizon at the assumed investment rate of 5%. When you do that, the chart looks like this:

	30-year mortgage	15-year mortgage
Interest rate	6%	5.5%
Investment rate of return	5%	5%
Interest expended	$231,676	$94,150
Tax savings	$69,503	$28,245
Tax savings invested	$187,944	$98,029
Net interest cost	$43,732	($3,879)
(Interest expended less tax savings invested)		

An interesting fact shows up here. In this example, the tax savings invested for the thirty-year time frame more than offsets the actual interest expended on the fifteen-year loan. In other words, over thirty years, the interest expended is recaptured via tax savings and returned to your wealth potential. This is a very important word: recaptured. In every financial decision, it is economically advisable to recapture as many costs as possible as you accumulate wealth.

Looking at net interest only, you would now favor the fifteen-year mortgage over the outlay of cash, even if you had the cash. In fifteen years, you would have completely covered the interest cost by the tax savings invested. But that is still not the entire story.

To get to an honest bottom line, you must carry all of the calculations out for the entire thirty years—not just the interest expended or the taxes saved, but also the outlays of monthly principal payments that are part of your monthly mortgage payments.

Notice that I have eliminated a couple of lines in the chart below:

1. I have replaced the interest expended with interest otherwise invested. I have done this because merely paying interest is not what is important. What is important is what you would have otherwise done with the money if you had not had a mortgage payment.

2. I've also eliminated the tax savings and more accurately accounted for the tax savings invested, as described above.

3. I've added an "all cash" column, and identified the "all cash" as a down payment. After all, isn't that what it is?

4. I've added a line to account for the principal payments made each year on your mortgage and assumed that you would have been able to invest that at 5% if you didn't own the home.

	All cash	30-year mortgage	15-year mortgage
Interest rate		6%	5.5%
Investment rate of return	5%	5%	5%
Interest otherwise invested		$626,480	$326,765
Tax savings invested		$187,944	$98,029
Down payment invested	$1,080,485	$216,097	$216,097
Monthly principal invested		$371,482	$596,489
Net cost to own home	$1,080,485	$1,026,115	$1,041,322

The bottom line in this example is that the most expensive way to purchase your home is with all cash; the best way to buy it is with a thirty-year mortgage. The difference is over $54,000—just in the way you purchase your home.

I purposely positioned the interest rates as close to each other as possible in order to illustrate that the principle of favoring the thirty-year mortgage most often is the best choice.

Individual circumstances may cause the analysis to differ. However, the greater the spread between the mortgage rate and the reinvestment rate, and the closer the spread between the interest rates of a fifteen-year and a thirty-year mortgage, the more dramatic the difference between your three choices will be.

Lesson #4: I was taught to pay off my mortgage as quickly as possible, but just the opposite is true.

So what if, rather than paying down the mortgage aggressively, you saved what you would have otherwise sent to the bank in a safe side fund? You would have the money to pay off the mortgage if you wanted to.

Lesson #5 (and a close corollary to Lesson #4): It is always more efficient to have the ability to pay off the mortgage with a safe side fund, just in case long-term economic factors change the analysis.

My conclusion regarding home ownership and the financing of your home is that your home is a place to grow your family, not your money.

The real opportunity, if you value pursuing the "best rate of return" perspective, comes from having as little of your own money as possible tied up in your home. This is because the rate of return on the equity in your home is 0%.

Consider two identical homes, one across the street from the other. They are both valued at $200,000. One is purchased with the minimum down payment of $40,000 (20%), and the other is purchased with a down payment of $100,000.

If the market value of each home increases by $10,000, each home is now worth $210,000. If the homes are sold, who gets the extra $10,000? Choose from the following possible answers.

a. All of the gain goes to the bank, since without its money you wouldn't have been able to own the home.

b. The money is shared with the mortgage bank, since it owns part of the home. In this situation, the home-owner of House 1 would receive $2,000 of the increase, and the homeowner of House 2 would receive $5,000, each increase representing the percentage of the homeowner's ownership.

c. Each of the homeowners will get the money.

Since the answer is each of the homeowners, the amount of equity in the home is extraneous information. Therefore, the rate of return on home equity is 0%. It doesn't matter how much equity is ascribed to the homeowner

I was always taught to calculate my rate of return on every investment. Even though I know my return on equity is 0%, let's do what I was taught, just to illustrate a point. In the gain of $10,000 on the $200,000 houses, remember that it didn't matter how much equity you had in the house; all of the gain was the homeowner's. But if you really want a rate of return, a $10,000 gain on a $100,000 investment is 10%, and on a $40,000 investment it is 25%. But remember, if you could have purchased the home with no down payment, a $10,000 gain on a $0 investment is an infinite rate of return. You can't get better than that! If you really want a rate of return, which would you rather have, 10%, 25%, or an infinite rate of return?

Lesson #6: I was taught to make as big a down payment as possible and establish as much of an equity position as soon as possible. Again, just the opposite is true; there is no investment value in an equity position. There is not even a minimal investment value in the equity of the house. The appreciation of the home's value is not dependent on your equity investment. Either the house appreciates or it doesn't. If it appreciates, the appreciated value is 100% the homeowner's profit, without regard to the amount of equity he or she has in the house.

In fact, one can argue that the larger your equity position, the more at risk you are.

Again, consider the two identical $200,000 homes. Not only are the two homes identical, but the family structures in each home are identical as well: a happily married couple with two grade school children. Both wives are radio personalities for the local radio station, and both husbands are top-notch reporters for the local newspaper. Their incomes are identical, and each income is necessary to pay the bills each month, including the mortgages.

The first couple, Mr. and Ms. Huge Debt, owes $160,000 on their home (they made the minimum down payment), and the second couple, Mr. and Ms. Max Down, owes $100,000 (they made a $100,000 down payment).

Assume further that both couples just inherited $90,000. What should they do with the money?

Believing in the logic of establishing as much equity in your home as possible, the Downs take the $90,000 to their local bank and pay the mortgage down to $10,000. To have as much equity in their home as possible, they have bought in so strongly that they have no other savings, other than in their "greatest asset." The Debts decide to buy a CD.

What happened to the Downs' mortgage payment? Was it reduced to reflect their $90,000 repayment? No, it remains the same; they will just pay off the mortgage that much faster, which falls right into their plans.

If Max suffers a career-ending disability, what happens to the Downs' ability to pay their mortgage? It suffers a big blow. Will the bank take into consideration that just a month before they brought in a check for $90,000? No! Will the bank take into consideration that they have been paying their mortgage on the bank's biweekly plan and are ahead on their mortgage by four months? No! What does the bank care about? It cares about the next month's mortgage payment being paid in full.

What happens when the mortgage check does not arrive? The Downs are assessed a late penalty, and their credit report takes a hit. What about when they can't make the payment in the second month of Max's disability? Same thing. What about the third month? A foreclosure sign goes up in the front yard!

What happens if, instead of a disability, there is a downturn in the economy, and the radio station uses all nationally syndicated shows and eliminates the local talent? Furthermore, the economic downturn results in a housing value decline of 25%. Now each home is worth only $150,000. Who is in the safer position? Huge Debt is upside down in his mortgage; he owes $160,000 on a home worth $150,000. Max Down feels pretty good; he owes just $10,000, even though his home has fallen in value.

The Downs are in trouble if they can't make the mortgage payment. Again, it is three strikes and they are out, and the bank feels pretty good about collecting the $10,000 mortgage balance from a home worth $150,000.

The Debts are a bit nervous. For them it is three strikes and they are out as well, but the bank is a bit reluctant to satisfy the $160,000 debt with the sale of the $150,000 house. Instead of foreclosing on the Debts' house, the bank agrees to waive the early withdrawal penalty on the $90,000 CD so that the Debts can continue to pay their mortgage.

Lesson #7: What I was taught to be true about my home being my best investment has turned out not to be true, because the lower your mortgage, the more at risk you are of losing your down payment or any other equity you have in the house, and the safer the bank is.

How wrong is the statement, "Your home is your most valuable asset"? Consider the following:

The thirty-year mortgage payment of $1,200 per month in the above example would have purchased a $250,000 asset (the house) and would be worth $606,000 if the home appreciated in value by 3% without any holding or improvement costs.

If a thirty-five-year-old couple could invest the $1,200 per month in a permanent life insurance contract, considered by most a stable and consistently growing asset, by the time they were sixty-five and ready to retire, projecting today's dividend rates, they would have $977,000 of cash value, representing equity to spend in retirement, and $2,000,000 of death benefits, representing the bricks and mortar of a house to leave to their children as their inheritance. The guarantees of an insurance policy are based on the claims-paying ability of the issuing insurance company.

These values would provide a tax-free retirement income of over $52,000 per year for the couple for twenty years in retirement and still leave at least $1,000,000 of assets to the next generation. Try getting that out of your reverse mortgage!

We start our lives chasing the American dream of owning our own home, our "most valuable asset." But when we understand the principles of this chapter, we find out that our "most valuable asset" is valuable not for the wealth it generates, but instead for the memories that develop as we raise our families. Houses were meant to be homes in which to raise families, not to store cash.

Asset Accumulation

It is said, "He who accumulates the most, wins the retirement race." Therefore, achieving the highest rate of return during your lifetime is the ultimate goal. Can you spend a rate of return? No! You can spend only cold, hard cash. So at the end of your life, as you look back, would you like to say you achieved the highest rate of return possible, or would you like to be able to say you enjoyed the highest level of spending possible?

The goal of asset accumulation is like setting out to climb Mt. Everest without any plan to get back down the other side. Is getting to the top the ultimate prize, or is it getting back down to tell about it?

Consider the following facts concerning the 29,035-foot peak of Mt. Everest. Between 1921 and 2006, 8,030 people set out to scale the mountain to the top. Some 2,250 were successful: a 28% success rate. Some would say that is a rate of success similar to that of those who truly achieve their retirement accumulation goals. That means 72% failed to get to the top. Most of them quit before the summit and successfully got back to base camp to tell their story of failure. Almost 3% failed the climb miserably; not only did they not get to the summit, but they didn't get back down, either. They died on the mountain. One hundred and twenty of them are still there. Of those who perished, 15% died on the way up; they never abandoned their climb, and they never came home to tell any stories. Seventy-three percent died on the way down; they simply did not abandon their climb early enough to sustain the descent. Now, the most startling statistic of them all is that 56% of those who perished on the mountainside perished after having succeeded in getting to the top! They died on the way back to base camp, after achieving their goal.

Just as in mountain climbing, asset accumulation is only half of the story; asset distribution is as important, if not more important.

Lesson #1: What I was taught to be true about asset accumulation has turned out not to be true, because it is more important to not run out of money during my lifetime than it is to accumulate the most.

There are two ways to distribute your retirement nest egg. Remember that the money has to last two lifetimes of a happily married couple.

The first and most conventional way to live out your retirement life is to take the approach of living on the interest only from your invested assets. This strategy is based on average rates of return, "buy term and invest the rest," and "Monte Carlo" simulations. Just how I wanted to live out my retirement—at the casino. Seems like a perfect match!

A Monte Carlo simulation merely takes the market rates of return, mixes up the returns, and looks at hundreds of random sets of return scenarios to establish the likelihood that you will outlast your money. Along with the random sets of returns, you test various rates of distribution.

Even a 5% withdrawal rate has a high risk of your principal decreasing. These last ten years are a good example, because there wasn't any strategy that would have sustained a 5% withdrawal based on a 5% return assumption.

Remember this chart from the "Be a Long-Term Investor" chapter? Starting with a $100,000 nest egg, and withdrawing 5% we see the following:

	Withdrawal	Rate of return	Beginning of the year	Gain/loss	End of the year
1999	-5,000	19.51%	95,000	18,535	113,535
2000	-5,000	-10.14%	108,535	-11,005	97,529
2001	-5,000	-13.04%	92,529	-12,066	80,463
2002	-5,000	-23.37%	75,463	-17,636	57,828
2003	-5,000	26.38%	52,828	13,936	66,763
2004	-5,000	8.99%	61,763	5,553	67,316
2005	-5,000	3.00%	62,316	1,869	64,185
2006	-5,000	13.62%	59,185	8,061	67,247
2007	-5,000	3.53%	62,247	2,197	64,444
2008	-5,000	-38.49%	59,444	-22,880	36,564

This illustrates that during this ten-year period, utilizing the Monte Carlo suggestion, 5% should sustain you. At the end of ten years, your principal has been reduced by almost two-thirds!

Even after you add back the market recovery years of 2009 and 2010, it is still not pretty.

	Withdrawal	Rate of return	Beginning of the year	Gain/loss	End of the year
1999	-5,000	19.51%	95,000	18,535	113,535
2000	-5,000	-10.14%	108,535	-11,005	97,529
2001	-5,000	-13.04%	92,529	-12,066	80,463
2002	-5,000	-23.37%	75,463	-17,636	57,828
2003	-5,000	26.38%	52,828	13,936	66,763
2004	-5,000	8.99%	61,763	5,553	67,316
2005	-5,000	3.00%	62,316	1,869	64,185
2006	-5,000	13.62%	59,185	8,061	67,247
2007	-5,000	3.53%	62,247	2,197	64,444
2008	-5,000	-38.49%	59,444	-22,880	36,564
2009	-5,000	23.49%	31,564	7,414	38,978
2010	-5,000	12.78%	33,978	4,342	38,320

Lesson #2: What I was taught to be true about asset accumulation has turned out not to be true, because as soon as you withdraw more than you earn, the downslope gets very steep and is hard to recover from.

Pretty amazing; you would think that a 23% and a 12% return would have reestablished much of the wealth lost in 2008. A good thing to remember is that the percentage losses in the stock market are calculated from larger numbers, making the actual dollar loss greater, and market gains are calculated on a smaller number, minimizing the dollar impact of a recovery.

The reason why no withdrawal strategy has worked in the last twelve years is that the only alternative to being invested in the market is to be invested in bonds or CDs. Only five times during the last twelve years were five-year CDs renewing at higher than

5%. I hope that you did not have a CD mature that needed to be renewed in 2011.

The mid-2011, five-year CD rate was 2.75% and falling every week. If you renewed at this rate and were withdrawing 5% from your account, you would be falling behind in each of the next five years. The only answer that the interest-only strategy can provide is for you to reduce your standard of living by 45%! What are you planning on cutting back on? Travel? Medical expenditures? Entertainment? Gifts to the grandchildren?

Here are the risks inherent to the interest-only approach:

1. Inflation: Since you are living off only the interest that the nest egg provides, you have a fixed amount of income. However, because inflation is eroding your purchasing power, you will likely experience a decrease in lifestyle.

2. Tax Rate: Since the government taxes the interest that you earn, you don't get to keep the entire amount of interest that is generated by the nest egg. What is the effect of the government raising the tax rates? You are still getting the same amount of income, but the government takes a larger share, so your spendable income is decreased.

3. Interest Rate: What happens to your income if the amount of interest you are earning decreases due to changes in the economy or the interest rate environment? Again, you experience a decrease in spendable income.

4. Loss of Capital: What happens if, either by choice or out of necessity, you have to invade your principal? Perhaps you have an unexpected medical expense, or

maybe you choose to help a child or grandchild with some money. Any amount of capital that you remove from your nest egg will affect the amount of interest that you will earn in the future, which will result in a decrease in spendable income.

5. Market Risk: In order to compensate for the first four risks, people choose to put a portion of their nest egg into the stock market, which introduces market risk into the equation.

Lesson #3: What I was taught to be true about asset accumulation has turned out not to be true, because there are major risks associated with living on just the interest my assets can provide.

Some of the obvious limits to the income-only approach are the following:

- The accumulation of assets is very important, since at retirement they must reach a certain level.

- Principal cannot be accessed deliberately for income.

- Fixed income for life provides no adjustment for inflation, resulting in a decrease of lifestyle every year.

The alternative approach is one in which you purposely consume some of your principal with the income strategy. The only reliable scenario for this approach is when there is a guaranteed death benefit equal to the beginning retirement asset balance for both spouses. The permanent death benefit guarantees that the principal spent in retirement together will be replaced for the surviving spouse. At this point in life, the life insurance is more about insuring your assets than your life. Without this safety net, you lack the permission slip to spend your principal. Do not choose the consume-principal approach to retirement income if you do not have this safety net. (Remember that the guaranteed death benefits of a life insurance contract are dependent on the claims-paying ability of the issuing life insurance company.)

Lesson #4: What I was taught to be true about asset accumulation has turned out not to be true, because there is no such thing as being "self-insured" with a retirement nest egg. There is a need for permanent life insurance in retirement. Perhaps better said, you will want permanent life insurance in retirement.

When the permission slip of life insurance is present during retirement, every asset is replenished at the first death, and the longer you live together in retirement, the less time one member of the happily married couple will live as a survivor. The longer you live, the more available the cash values are for consumption, allowing you to retire earlier, enhancing your lifestyle, or reducing the pressure on your accumulation assets to perform.

The key features of the "consumption of principal and interest" strategy are the following:

- As you spend down your principal, you have more money to enjoy your retirement.

- Your spouse's income is covered with your death benefit.

- Cash values of your life insurance policy provide you with less fear of running out of money.

Rather than having risks associated with this strategy, the risks associated with the income-only approach are mitigated.

1. Inflation: When you have the ability to consume your principal, you can mitigate inflation by taking out less money in the early years of retirement and then in-

creasing your distribution each year to keep up with inflation. The effect is that you can level your purchasing power.

2. Tax Rate: By spending some of your principal every year, you are reducing the size of your nest egg, which means there is less principal on which to earn interest in the succeeding years. As you earn less interest, you pay less tax. So, even if the tax rate increases in the future, there is less interest being earned, so it mitigates the impact of the tax increase.

3. Interest Rate: When you are consuming your own principal, a decrease in interest rate has less effect on your income than if you were trying to live on the interest alone.

4. Loss of Capital: You are already consuming your own capital, so, again, while it would impact your spendable income, you would still have more spendable income than if you were trying to live on only the interest.

5. Market Risk: You could actually eliminate market risk from this alternative, because you could construct a portfolio that would earn 2–3% return without exposing any of the assets to the market and, because of your ability to consume your principal, you would still have more income than living off interest alone.

Lesson #5: What I was taught to be true about asset accumulation has turned out not to be true, because while I may not *need* life insurance, I certainly *want* life insurance for the protection of my assets in my retirement.

Remember, the climb to the top is difficult and quite precarious, but the descent is fraught with even more obstacles, including those unseen and taken for granted as being safe. If something you thought to be true turned out not to be true, when would you want to know about it?

Financing Large Purchases

How you buy things may be the key to your secure financial future.

Every purchase, large or small, is a financing decision. As described in previous chapters, it is not just about interest charged on a purchase when you purchase with credit, but it is also about interest not earned if you use your own money.

What if you were the bank?

If you have any savings at all, you are the bank; you just don't know it. And because you don't know it, you don't treat yourself as a bank. If you treated yourself as a bank, you would pay yourself back for every purchase you made. That is not feasible, which is why we need to segment out purchases for consumption from purchases and expenses of larger items such as vehicles, college educations, homes, real estate taxes, and vacations. The list of pay-yourself-back purchases is personal and has infinite possibilities.

There are two keys to financial freedom, and both are related to your purchasing mentality.

1. Every time you make a purchase from your savings, pay yourself back.

2. Every time you have finished paying yourself back, keep paying yourself. Somehow, you figure how your

new monthly payment fits into your budget—just don't stop it; save it.

Let's first consider traditional bank financing, more specifically financing a large purchase such as a car. When you purchase a car and you use traditional financing, you have the choice of using your bank or credit union or the convenience of the dealership's financing options. Timing is the problem with bank financing; you first have to negotiate the purchase price of the car and then, at another location, negotiate the terms of your loan, and then bring the two together.

Many vehicle purchasers opt for the financing at the car dealership. Oftentimes the bank is not even considered, because the interest rate at the dealership is so low. In many circumstances you can find 1.9% or 2.9% financing rates. Sometimes you can even find a 0% loan. That is like free money! This is a close cousin to the three-year "same as cash" offers you find when you purchase furniture. The only difference is that the "same as cash" requires no payments until just before the term is over, and heaven forbid that you are a day late with your payment—all of the interest that accrued during the three years would be due. The 0% from the car dealership requires monthly payments.

The requirement of monthly payments is the first problem with the 0% loans. While the interest rate might be 0%, it still obligates you to a monthly payment that you might not be able to afford. I have worked with plenty of people who bought more car than they should have because the loan was "free."

Have you ever wondered why a car dealership can offer 0%? They can because 0% is often not 0%. Sometimes the 0% loan is the most profitable part of the new car purchase for the car dealership.

The small print of the 0% loan discloses that if you would rather not have the 0% loan, the dealership can offer you "cash back." A good example would be the purchase of a $30,000 car at 0% or $4,000 cash back.

The payment associated with financing $30,000 at 0% for four years would be $625 per month for forty-eight months. If you paid cash using your own personal bank, what is the real purchase price of the car? What is the amount of money you would need to give the car dealership when you take delivery of the car? The dealership would require the $30,000, less the $4,000 cash back. The real price of the car would be $26,000. If you financed yourself over the same time period at 0%, your payment to yourself would be $542 per month. So, for the same car, the car dealership is charging you over 15% more. This is because the car dealership isn't really loaning the money. They typically must prepay the financing incentive to the actual lending institution so that it can offer the 0% loan. They build the financing incentive into the higher price of the car. While there are other fees and charges that factor into the makeup of the 0% loan and higher purchase price for the car, another way to think about it is that the "cash back" you do not get when you choose the 0% loan is simply prepaid interest.

Lesson #1: What I was taught to be true about large purchase financing has turned out not to be true, because 0% is not 0% when it costs me more money.

Once again we are tricked by percentages, when we ought to be paying attention to our cash flows.

The next question is why do you finance the entire car when you don't consume the entire car? Why does the car dealership want to be repaid the entire $30,000 by the end of the fourth year, when the car may still have 50% of its value? It is because you are financing a purchase and not financing an asset.

If you were your own bank, couldn't you establish your own rules and require a repayment of only the value of the car you used during the given time frame? Of course you could. Assuming the car will still have $11,000 of value four years later, shouldn't you be paying back only $15,000? Paying yourself back $15,000 over four years, even at an 8% rate, your car payment to yourself would be $363. That is 42% less per month than what the car dealership is going to collect if you take the 0% loan, and you get to keep the interest. Can you think of any use you might have for $262 per month? The $262 per month invested or saved at 5% for a thirty-five-year-old until retirement thirty years later is almost $219,000 toward your retirement nest egg, as long as you find a suitable tax-free investment.

If you utilize the two keys to secure financial freedom stated above, this becomes real, actual money in your pocket.

Lesson #2: What I was taught to be true about large purchase financing has turned out not to be true, because you don't have to make monthly payments for the entire purchase price, only the portion you actually use, as long as you use yourself as a bank.

In the car example, you have restored $15,000 of the car value you used, and you still have a used car worth $11,000. Trade in the used car, couple that with another loan from yourself for $15,000, and purchase another $30,000 car ($30,000 less $4,000 cash back).

If you keep the discipline of saving an otherwise unnecessary monthly payment (because the loan was paid off) when you purchase the next car, you will be saving another $262 per month for twenty-six years at 5%. That will be another $168,000 for your retirement, as long as you find another tax-free investment or savings vehicle.

Lesson #3: I was taught that all consumer debt is bad debt, but that has turned out not to be true—not when you are the bank and treat yourself like the bank!

much money in our 401(k) plans and get our houses paid off as quickly as possible. Because we don't understand the rules, we are locked out of access to these stacks of money. When we look at our 401(k) plans, we hope someday they will come out of their growth slumbers and skyrocket just when we need it. But if the market soars, what will happen to interest rates? They may go up, and so will mortgage rates, effectively locking us out of accessing the cash stored in our houses.

You want to be in control of all of your money, and you won't be in control until you understand how important capital is. We start life using other people's capital and never learn to establish our own, because we are too quickly in the cycle of borrowing and too busy paying other people the interest they are due. If you were offered the opportunity to invest $10,000, but you had to have it by the end of the day, could you come up with it? Even if you could be guaranteed a 50% return by the end of the month? Your answer to this question will shed light on how well you understand the lesson of capital. You may have the money, but if it is spread out in places you can't get to, then it has lost its value as liquid capital.

Don't Get Discouraged

I recently watched one of my favorite movies, *Secretariat*. I like this movie because it illustrates the importance of planning our estates wisely. If not for the miraculous career of this once-in-a-lifetime racehorse, the estate of an entire family would have been wiped out by the estate taxes that were due.

Watching it this time, I was struck by the incredible career of the horse Sham, perhaps the greatest runner-up ever to run a race. Sham came in second in the very races that made Secretariat famous, except the last, the Belmont Stakes.

It was at the Belmont Stakes that Sham had the greatest chance. It was the longest race of the three jewels of the triple crown of horse racing. Sham was thought to have more stamina as a distance runner than as a sprinter. Secretariat, on the other hand, was a sprinter, and his value as a distance runner was the question of the day. Leading up to the race, as the movie points out, the last piece of direction Secretariat's trainer gave to the jockey was, "Run him hard, just don't burst his heart." Sometimes that is how we look at our investments. We run them hard, hoping not to burst the account; we don't know when to stop and get out. We burst the bubble.

In the case of Secretariat, he showed that distance was not a problem, and he beat the field by an incredible thirty-one lengths! His heart proved strong, and the horse that came in second was not Sham. It is said that it was Sham's heart that broke during the Belmont Stakes, as the horse lost to Secretariat by forty-five lengths, finished last, and never raced again. We must be careful whom we compare ourselves to. There will always be the story of the person who sprinted throughout his entire investment career and never looked back—an investment career as spectacular as the career of the great Secretariat. But those are once in a lifetime. Don't be discouraged by spectacular stories. Fight the fight, and finish the race.

Sprint Racing vs. Marathon Running

I'm also fascinated by the label "the fastest man on earth." This title goes to the person who runs the 100-meter dash faster than anyone else. Currently that title belongs to Usain Bolt, whose fastest time in the 100 meters is 9.58 seconds. At the other end of the spectrum is the marathon—26.2 miles. If math were the answer to all of life's challenges, to win the marathon, all you would need to do is divide 26.2 miles by 100 meters and get this guy to run the marathon 100 meters at a time. Obviously this won't work. Math isn't the answer.

The sprinter is done after 100 meters; he can't even go another 100 meters, much less 26 miles. A sprint is over quick. In a sprint you are always concerned with who is right behind you and wondering where you are now. People look at their money in the same way, always looking over their shoulder, wondering where they are now. A marathon is forward-looking, with an eye on the finish line 26 miles away. It doesn't really matter who is leading as the runners leave the starting line. Your money is marathon money, not sprint money. For a married couple both age sixty-five, it is likely that one of the spouses will live to see the age of ninety-two or more. That is a marathon! It doesn't matter much where you are after 100 meters. It is not how you leave the gate; it is how you finish. Marathon runners just want to establish a steady rate of speed that they can maintain over a long period of time. It is not how you start; it is how you finish.

Cash Value in the First Year

Life insurance cash values in the first year look much like marathon running. Getting out of the gate is not as important as finishing the race. Most of the time, what is deposited as the first year's premium is more than what is reported as your cash value. Cash value reflects only what you can recover from the policy if you choose to terminate it prematurely. It is no reflection of its long-term value. Therefore, when choosing a permanent life insurance contract, in the first year, never put money into the policy that you are going to need to access. That all begins to change in the second and third years, when the cash value is at least equal to your annual premium. In the most efficient permanent life insurance contracts, your lack of liquidity is only evident for a year at a time.

Hypothetically, let's suppose you put in $20,000. Let's further suppose that at the end of the year, you get a statement that says you have a cash value of $7,000. It appears you have lost $13,000. Your perception is correct, and if you chose to terminate the contract, you would indeed lose $13,000; but as long as you consider this a marathon run, the only thing you have actually lost is access to the $13,000, just as the only thing the marathon runner has lost is the prestige of being the early leader. Being the leader after the first mile is irrelevant; finishing first after the twenty-sixth mile is the objective. The only question you have to ask yourself is this: can you do without the use of that money?

It is an interesting question, because we rarely ask ourselves that question when we participate in our employer's 401(k) plan. In most situations, we lose access to that money until we reach fifty-nine and a half years of age, and only if we have terminated our employment with that employer after that age.

Instead, pretend you can start the policy in year two or three and look at the cash values in year two or three of the policy. In those years, your cash values can be equal to and greater than the amount of money you put in as your premium each year. The access to your cash value in the first year is limited for various reasons, including keeping the contract within the guidelines of the IRS's definition of life insurance. This is extremely important because compliance with the guidelines insures the tax benefits of a life insurance contract. If the contract falls outside of the guidelines, the tax benefits provided to the cash value part of the contract are forfeited, and the contract merely defers the taxes due on the growth of the contract, much like for an IRA. There is a big difference between deferring the taxes due to some uncertain date, at an uncertain rate, and deferring the use of the money a few years. Remember, you don't lose the money; you just defer the use of the money.

Reporting requirements are not the same for life insurance companies as they are for other financial institutions. What the life insurance company must show is only what is available. What would your 401(k) statement say if it had to disclose only what was available? If your 401(k) had a loan provision included in its design, it could show only 50% of the account value. If there were no loan provision or hardship withdrawal provision, it would have to show $0 until you turned fifty-nine and a half, and still footnote the statement indicating that you had to terminate your job first.

Remember that in your permanent life insurance contract, you are entitled to more than the cash values. Your heirs are entitled to death benefits if you should meet with an untimely and unanticipated early death. Another way of looking at the loss of liquidity in the first year is to consider the opportunity cost of this loss over the same time frame you would have had to supplement your estate with an equal amount of death benefits through a term insurance policy. Let's consider that you are a thirty-five-year-old husband and father of a young family. To permanently forgo access to $13,000 in the first year of the policy at 5% is $56,000 for thirty years to age sixty-five. The cost for an equal amount of term insurance at 5% opportunity is $142,000. Which opportunity cost would you like to incur: $56,000 that you will have completely recaptured in your cash values at age sixty-five, or $142,000 that the life insurance company will keep forever?

Remember that you are in a marathon run, not a sprint race.

Accumulation vs. Distribution vs. Generational Transfers

Financial strategies are completely different depending on whether you are on the accumulation side of life or the distribution side of life. The most dramatic financial tool for accumulation is likely the worst financial tool when it comes to distribution. That is not to say that you should avoid the qualified plan—401(k), IRA, or anything in which you receive a deduction from taxable income when you make your deposits—but it should be used in such a way as to have options when you take distributions from this tool for retirement. The overuse of a qualified plan may result in retiring in a higher tax bracket than the tax bracket that was used to calculate the tax savings when the contribution was made. Getting the money out in the lowest tax bracket is the key, which may be sooner in retirement than you think!

Furthermore, when estates transfer from one generation to another, another set of rules is set into motion. A bountiful amount of money is about to be left to the baby boomer generation. Distributions at death are different under certain circumstances. Get ready now. Know how qualified plans, mutual funds, and life insurance, just to name a few, are treated, and structure their ownership and inheritance rights now. How you allocate is very important. As an example, qualified plan money left to a charity in your estate is not taxable to the charity; however, it is taxable to your children at their tax rates if they inherit this money.

In retirement and at death, it is more about the strategy than the financial product. You may have been product-intensive throughout your accumulation life; now it is all about strategy to access it. The sooner you move to managing your money strategically rather than purchasing the hot product, the better off your distribution years will be.

A Golf Analogy

When you start to shift your thinking from focusing on the best financial product to following the best financial strategy, you begin to understand that a number of clubs are necessary to play the game. In golf you are allowed only fourteen clubs. The one that gets the most attention and is practiced with the most at the range is the one that hits the ball the farthest: the driver. The driver is always the most replaced club in the bag, as we try to find the newest and best driver to hit the ball farther. Hit it hard, and hit it far. However, hitting it hard and far is fraught with risk. Rough, water, sand, and out-of-bounds stakes are just waiting for your ball. You don't always end up in the fairway, but it does go far. It feels really good when you swing the driver just right. The driver is great, but the best club in the bag is the putter. You use the putter on every hole; the driver is left in the bag on several holes and is usually taken out of the bag only fourteen times, if that often.

The pros know that you swing the driver for show and you putt for dough. Master the putter, and you will cash more championship checks. In your finances, the driver is your accumulation tool, but if you want to get the most money out of your assets, you need to master the putter. Permanent life insurance is the putter, because it enhances many accumulation products. It can also save an errant financial start, just as a putter can save par after an errant drive. Obviously it is not the only product in the bag. You need all of the others. But you can't get through a game without a putter. Unfortunately, many of us try.

Accuracy is more important than distance on the green. The putter is the peak performer.

Get Your Social Security in a Lump Sum

What?

And tax-free?

Oh, come on, now!

Most people become very disappointed when they finally retire and realize that because of the way they saved for retirement, they are going to have to pay taxes on social security income.

By the time that retirement rolls around, most people have their homes paid off. The good news is that you no longer have a house payment, but the bad news, as shown in previous chapters, is that all of the equity in the house is earning 0% and is completely unusable. The retirement plan is to make the house the children's inheritance and live off social security and your 401(k). Excessive distributions from a 401(k) require you to pay income taxes on your social security. "Excessive" is defined by the IRS as $32,000 for a married couple and $25,000 for a single individual or marriage survivor (2010 definitions).

Excessive? How do you avoid this unfortunate surprise? Let's say your social security income is $1,500 per month and you own a home worth $300,000 without a mortgage debt. If you were able to obtain a conventional thirty-year mortgage, with 20% down, your mortgage payment would be $1,432 at 6%. What does this achieve? If you use your taxable social security payment of $1,500 each month to pay your deductible mortgage payment of $1,432, you would end up with an excess $68 each month and a lump sum of $240,000 tax-free. To be completely clear, the

$240,000 comes from the loan proceeds of the mortgage and is a tax-free distribution; the taxes on the social security income are offset by the interest paid on the mortgage.

The best application of this strategy is someone who doesn't really need social security to live on. And instead of waiting until that someone dies to give the kids the value of the home, he or she can give an early inheritance while still living. Why wait till death to give your heirs the value of your home?

This is just one example of utilizing a retirement distribution strategy rather than an investment product. This example illustrates the power of not leaving your wealth in your home; all you have to do is talk with the survivors of natural disasters for it to really hit home.

Disaster Lessons

A natural disaster comes most unexpectedly, even if we live in disaster-prone areas. Whether you are victimized by a broad-brush natural disaster such as a hurricane, flood, forest fire, or earthquake, or you live through a more local disaster such as a tornado or personal fire, if your money is stored in your paid-off house, your disaster may just be beginning. Don't get me wrong—I believe that your house should be paid off, but the value should be in a safe side account, and you should still be carrying a mortgage.

Under any of the above disasters, assume your paid-off house is totally demolished. The flood or earthquake coverage maximum may be significantly less than the value of the house, or you may have a financially significant deductible. If all of your money is being stored in your house, where is the money that you need to rebuild? A $250,000 limit will rebuild only half of the $500,000 house.

What if there was a mortgage? The insurance maximum is still only half of what it will cost to rebuild, but the bank is now on a major hook as well as you. And the bank has major legal resources behind the insurance loss. The bank may not be able to work it out, but do you really want to have to wait for the insurance company to sort it all out? In a broad-based disaster, you are not the only claim. Money in a safe side account that could have been used to pay off the mortgage would be available to begin the rebuilding process in a safe environment until the insurance mess is all sorted out.

What if it is your business that is destroyed? Now more than just your life has been disrupted. But with the money in a safe side account and not in the bricks and mortar, you can be back in business and not have to wait on the insurance company. Employees are re-employed. Customers remain loyal. Money tied up is not very usable. Money available is king.

If you are forced to rebuild, access to capital is a very comforting feeling. Unfortunately, too many of us have to live through it to understand it. This last statement is illustrated by the mayor of Port Arthur, Texas, whose home survived Hurricane Rita only to be destroyed in the aftermath by fire. In his interview, he didn't say, "Boy, I'm sure glad we just paid off our house." Instead he said, "The worst part is that we just paid off the house last month." If his home was a safe place to store his cash, why would that be the worst part?

One Last Example of Having a Strategy of Coordinating Financial Products

If you are interested in tax-deferred growth, it is available in more than qualified plans. What do you like best about your 401(k) plan? If you are like some, you will say, "I'm saving all of those taxes." Now you know that is an untrue statement. You are not saving taxes, just deferring them to the future at a time in which you don't know at what rate your savings will be taxed. If you like tax-deferred growth, how are you enjoying your 401(k)? Do you have fond conversations about it with your spouse and family? What do the kids think about your 401(k)? They don't know anything about it? What do you mean, you are putting all of that money in your 401(k), but you can't enjoy it for thirty years?

Why not put the money somewhere where you can enjoy it and still have it grow? How about on the beach or in the mountains? Like to ski, fish, enjoy the outdoors? Wouldn't it be nice to put that thirty-years-from-now money somewhere where you can enjoy it today?

A second home in the mountains or a condo on the beach gives you similar tax-deferral opportunities to those of your 401(k) plan. Your 401(k) deferral is tax-deferred, and your second home's mortgage interest is tax-deductible. From a tax deduction perspective, there is no difference—you are not paying current taxes on the income used for either the retirement plan deferral or the interest paid. The 401(k) is supposed to increase in value—does it? The real estate property is supposed to increase in value—can it? Perhaps it can, more so than before, ever since the meltdown of the real estate values.

In what other ways does a vacation condo compare to a 401(k)?

1. At retirement, both will need to be liquidated to finance your retirement. The sales proceeds of the 401(k) are taxed at ordinary income tax rates, and the sales proceeds of the condo are taxed at more favorable capital gains rates.

2. At death, both will pass on to the next generation. The 401(k) will be taxed at ordinary income tax rates, and the condo will be income tax-free upon its sale, since investments receive a step up in basis for the heirs at the owner's death. There may be estate tax considerations, however, as there are with every asset.

3. You are limited to how much you put into your 401(k) plan. You can deduct the interest on a loan up to $1,000,000 for the purchase of your condo.

4. With your 401(k), you get annual statements; with your condo, you get annual pictures of your family vacation to review.

5. Your 401(k) gives you no enjoyment during your working career; your condo gives you a lifetime of memories.

6. You are locked out of your 401(k) until you are fifty-nine and a half, but with your condo you get two sets of front-door keys.

7. If you use your 401(k) early, you are penalized; if you use your condo early, not can you only receive immeasurable opportunities for your family, but you can also share them with your friends and your kid's friends.

8. With your 401(k), even if you don't need it, you have to begin liquidating it at age seventy and a half; with your condo, if you don't need it, you can always give it away to another family member.

When you are planning your finances, think outside of the box. Just make sure to weigh all of the advantages and disadvantages of your options. There is not just one magic product, but with your imagination and creativity, anything is possible.

What I Believe

I believe ...

1. The financial decision-making process is more important than any product available.

2. Everyone ought to be out of debt. The probability of financial success is greatly enhanced if you are debt-free.

3. There is a minimum amount one ought to be saving.

4. People ought to know where they are today. How are you doing financially?

5. People are entitled to know if they will be financially successful if they keep doing what they are doing.

6. People are transferring their money away unnecessarily. People ought to know where this is happening.

7. Cash values are more valuable than home equity.

8. Your mortgage should be paid off as quickly as possible.

9. Your mortgage is paid off when you have the money to pay it off, not when you terminate the mortgage contract.

10. Taxable income from assets that are in a taxable environment for a long period of time has a devastating effect on your ability to accumulate money.

11. Opportunity cost is a real thing. If you lose a dollar, you not only lose the dollar but also what that dollar could have earned over time.

12. Qualified plans defer the tax *and* the tax calculation to some uncertain time, at some uncertain rate.

13. The number-one concern of people approaching retirement is running out of money.

14. People approaching retirement want to talk to someone about the issues confronting them.

15. Over the next twenty-five years, distribution strategies will be more important than accumulation strategies for most Americans.

Afterthoughts

One of the most difficult things to do is to describe some-where you have visited that can't be described with words. Sometimes when I meet with clients and try to explain these concepts, words just don't do it. But it is more than satisfying when clients have embraced the concepts and have experienced the results so much so that they refer their friends with enthusiasm.

It is very much like having visited one of our great national parks, whether that is Yellowstone, Grand Teton, Mount Rushmore, the Grand Canyon, Yosemite, the Appalachian Trail, the Great Smoky Mountains, or the Pacific National Monument, including Pearl Harbor. The experience is the same; your words or even the pictures you take just don't do it justice. The best way to explain the experience is to take the members of your audience with you the next time you go, and watch their facial expressions and body language as they experience what you have been trying to tell them.

If you embrace and apply the principles contained in this book, you will have the same experience I have had. I wish I could be there to see your face!